SQUIRES KITCHEN'S
organiser

Personal Notes

Name

Home address

Home telephone   Mobile

Personal email

Business address

Work telephone   Work email

Doctor telephone

Blood group   Allergies

In case of emergency, please call: Name

Telephone

First published in October 2011 by
B. Dutton Publishing Limited, The Grange,
Hones Yard, Farnham, Surrey, GU9 8BB.

Publisher: Beverley Dutton

Editor: Jenny Stewart

Art Director/Designer: Sarah Ryan

Deputy Editor: Jenny Royle

Designer: Zena Manicom

Sub Editor/Graphic Designer: Louise Pepé

PR and Advertising Manager: Natalie Bull

Editorial Assistant: Amy Norman

Photography: Alister Thorpe and Rob Goves

Printed in China

January

1st	New Year's Day
	New Year Holiday (UK and Republic of Ireland)
3rd	New Year Holiday (Scotland)
23rd	Chinese (Lunar) New Year
25th	Robert Burns Night
27th	Holocaust Memorial Day

February

6th	60th Anniversary of Accession of Queen Elizabeth II
14th	St. Valentine's Day
21st	Shrove Tuesday
22nd	Ash Wednesday

March

1st	St. David's Day
5th-8th	Squires Kitchen's International 4 Day School
9th-11th	Squires Kitchen's 26th Annual Exhibition, Farnham
12th-16th	Squires Kitchen's International 5 Day School
12th	Commonwealth Day
17th	St. Patrick's Day
18th	Mothering Sunday
19th	Bank Holiday (Northern Ireland); Holiday (Republic of Ireland)
21st-25th	Country Living Magazine Spring Fair
25th	British Summer Time begins

April

1st	Palm Sunday
5th	Maundy Thursday
6th	Good Friday (UK)
7th	Jewish Passover
8th	Easter Sunday
9th	Easter Monday (UK and Republic of Ireland)
21st	BSG Durham Branch Exhibition, St. Leonard's Catholic School, Durham
23rd	St. George's Day

May

7th	May Day Holiday (UK and Republic of Ireland)
8th	World Red Cross Day
19th-20th	BSG 7th International Exhibition, The International Centre, Telford
	Cake Design Italian Festival, Milan

June

2nd-5th	The Queen's Diamond Jubilee
4th	Holiday (Republic of Ireland)
13th-17th	BBC Good Food Show Summer, NEC Birmingham
17th	Father's Day
21st	Longest Day
30th	Armed Forces Day

July

12th	Holiday (Northern Ireland)
27th	London 2012 Olympic Games start

August

6th	Holiday (Scotland, Republic of Ireland)
27th	Late Summer Holiday (UK)

September

8th-9th	2nd Squires Kitchen Exposition, Vinci Centre, Tours, France
17th	Jewish New Year
22nd	Autumnal Equinox
26th	Jewish Day of Atonement

October

24th	United Nations Day
26th-28th	BBC Good Food Show Scotland, SECC Glasgow
28th	British Summer Time ends
29th	Holiday (Republic of Ireland)
31st	Hallowe'en

November

1st	All Saints' Day
5th	Guy Fawkes Night
9th-11th	International Cake Show, NEC Birmingham
	MasterChef Live, Olympia Exhibition Centre, London
11th	Remembrance Sunday
15th	Muslim New Year (provisional)
21st-25th	BBC Good Food Show Winter, NEC Birmingham
30th	St. Andrew's Day

December

2nd	First Sunday of Advent
21st	Shortest Day
25th	Christmas Day; Holiday (UK and Republic of Ireland)
26th	Boxing Day (UK); Holiday (UK and Republic of Ireland)
	St. Stephen's Day (Republic of Ireland)

It's easy to order online from Squires Kitchen!   www.squires-shop.com   www.squires-shop.es    www.squires-shop.fr

Edible flowers for cake decorating

Edible flowers are safe to use directly on cakes as a decoration: make sure chemicals haven't been used in their cultivation, wash them first and check which parts of the flowers or leaves are edible before eating them.

Anchusa

Antirrhinum

Bergamot

Borage

Broad bean flowers

Carnations

Chamomile

Chervil

Chives

Chrysanthumum (petals)

Clove pinks

Common daisy

Cornflower

Courgette, squash, marrow and pumpkin flowers

Cowslip

Dandelion

Daylily

Dianthus

Elderflower

Garlic chives

Honeysuckle

Lavender

Lilac

Marigolds

Nasturtium (flowers and leaves)

Pansy

Pea flower

Primrose

Rocket

Rose

Rose geranium (flowers and leaves)

Sprouting broccoli, cauliflower and mustard flowers

Sweet cicely

Tulip

Violet

Year-round flowers

Sugar flower by Paddi Clark

If you are making sugar flowers for wedding cakes it is useful to know which flowers are in season. A list of popular seasonal flowers is given on the Monthly Planner. Flowers that are available all year round include:

Anthurium	Euphorbia
Anemone	Freesia
Carnation	Gerbera
Chrysanthemum	Lily of the valley
Daisy	Orchid

Anniversaries

Traditional and modern gift ideas and flowers associated with anniversaries.

	Traditional	Modern	Flowers
1st	Paper	Clocks, plastic	Pansy
2nd	Cotton	China	Cosmos
3rd	Leather	Crystal, glass	Fuchsia
4th	Fruit, flowers	Electrical appliances	Geranium
5th	Wood	Silverware	Daisy
6th	Sugar, iron	Wood	Calla lily
7th	Wool, copper	Desk set	Jack-in-the-pulpit
8th	Bronze, pottery	Lace, linen	Clematis
9th	Pottery, willow	Leather	Poppy
10th	Tin, aluminium	Diamond jewellery	Daffodil
11th	Steel	Fashion jewellery	Morning glory
12th	Silk, fine linen	Colour gems, pearls	Peony
13th	Lace	Furs, textiles	Hollyhock
14th	Ivory	Gold jewellery	Dahlia
15th	Crystal	Watches	Rose
20th	China	Bone china, platinum	Day lily
25th	Silver	Silver	Iris
30th	Pearl	Diamond jewellery	Sweet pea
35th	Coral	Jade	N/A
40th	Ruby	Ruby	Nasturtium
45th	Sapphire	Sapphire	N/A
50th	Gold	Gold	Violet
55th	Emerald	Emerald	N/A
60th	Diamond	Diamond	N/A
70th	Platinum, Diamond	Platinum	N/A
75th	Diamond	Diamond	N/A

1 Sunday

2 Monday

3 Tuesday

4 Wednesday

5 Thursday

6 Friday

7 Saturday

8 Sunday

9 Monday

10 Tuesday

11 Wednesday

12 Thursday

13 Friday

14 Saturday

15 Sunday

16 Monday

17 Tuesday

18 Wednesday

19 Thursday

20 Friday

21 Saturday

22 Sunday

23 Monday

24 Tuesday

25 Wednesday

26 Thursday

27 Friday

28 Saturday

29 Sunday

30 Monday

31 Tuesday

Seasonal Flowers

Alstroemeria
Amaryllis
Aster
Astilbe
Chinese lantern
Heather
Hellebore
Lilac
Mimosa
Narcissus
Tulip
Waxflower

Sugar flowers by Paddi Clark

S	M	T	W	T	F	S
1	2	3	4	5	6	7
8	9	10	11	12	13	14
15	16	17	18	19	20	21
22	23	24	25	26	27	28
29	30	31				

1 Wednesday

2 Thursday

3 Friday

4 Saturday

5 Sunday

6 Monday

7 Tuesday

8 Wednesday

9 Thursday

10 Friday

11 Saturday

12 Sunday

13 Monday

14 Tuesday

15 Wednesday

16 Thursday

17 Friday

18 Saturday

19 Sunday

20 Monday

21 Tuesday

22 Wednesday

23 Thursday

24 Friday

25 Saturday

26 Sunday

27 Monday

28 Tuesday

29 Wednesday

Seasonal Flowers

Amaryllis
Bouvardia
Daffodil
Euphorbia
Iris
Ivy
Lavender
Mimosa
Nerine
Primula
Reticulata
Sweet pea
Sunflower
Violet
Waxflower

Sugar flowers by Paddi Clark

S	M	T	W	T	F	S
			1	2	3	4
5	6	7	8	9	10	11
12	13	14	15	16	17	18
19	20	21	22	23	24	25
26	27	28	29			

1 Thursday

2 Friday

3 Saturday

4 Sunday

5 Monday

6 Tuesday

7 Wednesday

8 Thursday

9 Friday

10 Saturday

11 Sunday

12 Monday

13 Tuesday

14 Wednesday

15 Thursday

16 Friday

17 Saturday

18 Sunday

19 Monday

20 Tuesday

21 Wednesday

22 Thursday

23 Friday

24 Saturday

25 Sunday

26 Monday

27 Tuesday

28 Wednesday

29 Thursday

30 Friday

31 Saturday

Seasonal Flowers

Amaryllis
Aster
Astilbe
Bluebell
Bouvardia
Camellia
Cherry blossom
Forget-me-not
Gypsophila
Hyacinth
Iris
Mimosa
Narcissus
Poppy
Stock

Sugar flowers by Paddi Clark

S	M	T	W	T	F	S
				1	2	3
4	5	6	7	8	9	10
11	12	13	14	15	16	17
18	19	20	21	22	23	24
25	26	27	28	29	30	31

1 Sunday	
2 Monday	
3 Tuesday	
4 Wednesday	
5 Thursday	
6 Friday	
7 Saturday	
8 Sunday	
9 Monday	
10 Tuesday	
11 Wednesday	
12 Thursday	
13 Friday	
14 Saturday	
15 Sunday	
16 Monday	
17 Tuesday	
18 Wednesday	
19 Thursday	
20 Friday	
21 Saturday	
22 Sunday	
23 Monday	
24 Tuesday	
25 Wednesday	
26 Thursday	
27 Friday	
28 Saturday	
29 Sunday	
30 Monday	

Seasonal Flowers

Agapanthus
Allium
Alstroemeria
Amaryllis
Antirrhinum
Aster
Bouvardia
Cornflower
Crocus
Daffodils
Delphinium
Gypsophila
Iris
Mimosa
Nigella
Peony
Poppy
Ranunculus
Stock
Sweet pea
Tulip

Sugar flowers by Paddi Clark

S	M	T	W	T	F	S
1	2	3	4	5	6	7
8	9	10	11	12	13	14
15	16	17	18	19	20	21
22	23	24	25	26	27	28
29	30					

1 Tuesday

2 Wednesday

3 Thursday

4 Friday

5 Saturday

6 Sunday

7 Monday

8 Tuesday

9 Wednesday

10 Thursday

11 Friday

12 Saturday

13 Sunday

14 Monday

15 Tuesday

16 Wednesday

17 Thursday

18 Friday

19 Saturday

20 Sunday

21 Monday

22 Tuesday

23 Wednesday

24 Thursday

25 Friday

26 Saturday

27 Sunday

28 Monday

29 Tuesday

30 Wednesday

31 Thursday

Seasonal Flowers

Agapanthus
Allium
Alstroemeria
Amaryllis
Antirrhinum
Aster
Astilbe
Bouvardia
Camellia
Cherry blossom
Cornflower
Delphinium
Echinop
Gypsophila
Lisianthus
Mimosa
Nigella
Peony
Poppy
Stock
Waxflower

Sugar flowers by Paddi Clark

S	M	T	W	T	F	S
		1	2	3	4	5
6	7	8	9	10	11	12
13	14	15	16	17	18	19
20	21	22	23	24	25	26
27	28	29	30	31		

1 Friday

2 Saturday

3 Sunday

4 Monday

5 Tuesday

6 Wednesday

7 Thursday

8 Friday

9 Saturday

10 Sunday

11 Monday

12 Tuesday

13 Wednesday

14 Thursday

15 Friday

16 Saturday

17 Sunday

18 Monday

19 Tuesday

20 Wednesday

21 Thursday

22 Friday

23 Saturday

24 Sunday

25 Monday

26 Tuesday

27 Wednesday

28 Thursday

29 Friday

30 Saturday

Seasonal Flowers

Allium
Antirrhinum
Aster
Astilbe
Bouvardia
Cornflower
Delphinium
Echinop
Forget-me-not
Gardenia
Gypsophila
Iris
Lavender
Lily
Mimosa
Nigella
Peony
Sweet pea
Sweet William

Sugar flowers by Paddi Clark

S	M	T	W	T	F	S
					1	2
3	4	5	6	7	8	9
10	11	12	13	14	15	16
17	18	19	20	21	22	23
24	25	26	27	28	29	30

1 Sunday

2 Monday

3 Tuesday

4 Wednesday

5 Thursday

6 Friday

7 Saturday

8 Sunday

9 Monday

10 Tuesday

11 Wednesday

12 Thursday

13 Friday

14 Saturday

15 Sunday

16 Monday

17 Tuesday

18 Wednesday

19 Thursday

20 Friday

21 Saturday

22 Sunday

23 Monday

24 Tuesday

25 Wednesday

26 Thursday

27 Friday

28 Saturday

29 Sunday

30 Monday

31 Tuesday

Seasonal Flowers

Agapanthus
Allium
Aster
Astilbe
Bouvardia
Cornflower
Delphinium
Echinop
Forget-me-not
Iris
Lavender
Marguerite
Marigold
Mimosa
Nigella
Peony
Phlox
Stock
Sunflower

Sugar flowers by Paddi Clark

S	M	T	W	T	F	S
1	2	3	4	5	6	7
8	9	10	11	12	13	14
15	16	17	18	19	20	21
22	23	24	25	26	27	28
29	30	31				

1 Wednesday

2 Thursday

3 Friday

4 Saturday

5 Sunday

6 Monday

7 Tuesday

8 Wednesday

9 Thursday

10 Friday

11 Saturday

12 Sunday

13 Monday

14 Tuesday

15 Wednesday

16 Thursday

17 Friday

18 Saturday

19 Sunday

20 Monday

21 Tuesday

22 Wednesday

23 Thursday

24 Friday

25 Saturday

26 Sunday

27 Monday

28 Tuesday

29 Wednesday

30 Thursday

31 Friday

Seasonal Flowers

Aster
Dahlia
Gladioli
Larkspur
Poppy
Sweet pea
September
Late sunflower
Lavender
Love lies bleeding
Nerine
Ornamental cabbage

Sugar flowers by Paddi Clark

S	M	T	W	T	F	S
			1	2	3	4
5	6	7	8	9	10	11
12	13	14	15	16	17	18
19	20	21	22	23	24	25
26	27	28	29	30	31	

1 Saturday

2 Sunday

3 Monday

4 Tuesday

5 Wednesday

6 Thursday

7 Friday

8 Saturday

9 Sunday

10 Monday

11 Tuesday

12 Wednesday

13 Thursday

14 Friday

15 Saturday

16 Sunday

17 Monday

18 Tuesday

19 Wednesday

20 Thursday

21 Friday

22 Saturday

23 Sunday

24 Monday

25 Tuesday

26 Wednesday

27 Thursday

28 Friday

29 Saturday

30 Sunday

Seasonal Flowers

Agapanthus
Dahlia
Gladiolius
Gloriosa
Hydrangea
Lavender
Sunflower
Love lies bleeding
Nerine

Sugar flowers by Paddi Clark

S	M	T	W	T	F	S
30						1
2	3	4	5	6	7	8
9	10	11	12	13	14	15
16	17	18	19	20	21	22
23	24	25	26	27	28	29

1 Monday

2 Tuesday

3 Wednesday

4 Thursday

5 Friday

6 Saturday

7 Sunday

8 Monday

9 Tuesday

10 Wednesday

11 Thursday

12 Friday

13 Saturday

14 Sunday

15 Monday

16 Tuesday

17 Wednesday

18 Thursday

19 Friday

20 Saturday

21 Sunday

22 Monday

23 Tuesday

24 Wednesday

25 Thursday

26 Friday

27 Saturday

28 Sunday

29 Monday

30 Tuesday

31 Wednesday

Seasonal Flowers

Astilbe
Celosia
Cockscomb
Hypericum
Pink

Sugar flowers by Paddi Clark

S	M	T	W	T	F	S
	1	2	3	4	5	6
7	8	9	10	11	12	13
14	15	16	17	18	19	20
21	22	23	24	25	26	27
28	29	30	31			

1 Thursday

2 Friday

3 Saturday

4 Sunday

5 Monday

6 Tuesday

7 Wednesday

8 Thursday

9 Friday

10 Saturday

11 Sunday

12 Monday

13 Tuesday

14 Wednesday

15 Thursday

16 Friday

17 Saturday

18 Sunday

19 Monday

20 Tuesday

21 Wednesday

22 Thursday

23 Friday

24 Saturday

25 Sunday

26 Monday

27 Tuesday

28 Wednesday

29 Thursday

30 Friday

Seasonal Flowers

Amaryllis
Lisianthus
Snowdrop

Cold porcelain flowers
by Janet Carpenter

S	M	T	W	T	F	S
				1	2	3
4	5	6	7	8	9	10
11	12	13	14	15	16	17
18	19	20	21	22	23	24
25	26	27	28	29	30	

1 Saturday

2 Sunday

3 Monday

4 Tuesday

5 Wednesday

6 Thursday

7 Friday

8 Saturday

9 Sunday

10 Monday

11 Tuesday

12 Wednesday

13 Thursday

14 Friday

15 Saturday

16 Sunday

17 Monday

18 Tuesday

19 Wednesday

20 Thursday

21 Friday

22 Saturday

23 Sunday

24 Monday

25 Tuesday

26 Wednesday

27 Thursday

28 Friday

29 Saturday

30 Sunday

31 Monday

Seasonal Flowers

Dutch hyacinth
Narcissus
Passion flower

Sugar flowers by Paddi Clark

S	M	T	W	T	F	S
30	31					1
2	3	4	5	6	7	8
9	10	11	12	13	14	15
16	17	18	19	20	21	22
23	24	25	26	27	28	29

black forest indulgence cake

edibles

65g (2¼oz) butter

75g (2½oz) SK Dark Couverture Chocolate

125ml (4½fl oz) golden syrup

175g (6¼oz) self-raising flour

65g (2¼oz) light brown sugar

25g (1oz) cocoa powder

3ml (½tsp) baking powder

1 egg

100g (3½oz) chopped, semi-dried cherries

500ml (17½fl oz) Chantilly cream

200g (7¼oz) freshly poached cherries

equipment

Large bowl

Electric mixer

20.5cm (8") round cake tin, lined with greaseproof paper

1 Preheat the oven to 180°C/350°F/gas mark 4.

2 Place the butter, chocolate and golden syrup into a large bowl and add 250ml of boiling water. Mix until combined.

3 Place the flour, cocoa powder, sugar and baking powder in an electric mixer with the paddle attachment.

4 Add the egg and start mixing on a slow speed. Slowly add the chocolate mixture and mix until it becomes a smooth paste. Add some chopped, semi-dried cherries to the sponge at the end of mixing.

5 Place the mixture into a lined cake tin and bake for 45-50 minuets or until a skewer inserted in the centre comes out clean. When baked, remove from the oven and allow to cool completely.

6 When the cake is cool, fill with Chantilly cream and freshly poached cherries.

Mark Tilling

26
Monday • Lundi • Lunes

27
Tuesday • Mardi • Martes

28
Wednesday • Mercredi • Miércoles

29
Thursday • Jeudi • Jueves

30
Friday • Vendredi • Viernes

31
Saturday • Samedi • Sábado

1
Sunday • Dimanche • Domingo

New Year's Day

Notes

2
Monday • Lundi • Lunes

New Year Holiday
(UK and Republic of Ireland)

3
Tuesday • Mardi • Martes

New Year Holiday (Scotland)

4
Wednesday • Mercredi
• Miércoles

5
Thursday • Jeudi • Jueves

6
Friday • Vendredi • Viernes

7
Saturday • Samedi • Sábado

8
Sunday • Dimanche
• Domingo

Notes

January						
S	M	T	W	T	F	S
1	2	3	4	5	6	7
8	9	10	11	12	13	14
15	16	17	18	19	20	21
22	23	24	25	26	27	28
29	30	31				

9
Monday • Lundi • Lunes

10
Tuesday • Mardi • Martes

11
Wednesday • Mercredi
• Miércoles

12
Thursday • Jeudi • Jueves

13
Friday • Vendredi • Viernes

14
Saturday • Samedi • Sábado

15
Sunday • Dimanche
• Domingo

Notes

16
Monday • Lundi • Lunes

17
Tuesday • Mardi • Martes

18
Wednesday • Mercredi • Miércoles

19
Thursday • Jeudi • Jueves

20
Friday • Vendredi • Viernes

21
Saturday • Samedi • Sábado

22
Sunday • Dimanche • Domingo

Notes

January

S	M	T	W	T	F	S
1	2	3	4	5	6	7
8	9	10	11	12	13	14
15	16	17	18	19	20	21
22	23	24	25	26	27	28
29	30	31				

23
Monday • Lundi • Lunes

Chinese (Lunar) New Year

24
Tuesday • Mardi • Martes

25
Wednesday • Mercredi • Miércoles

Robert Burns Night

26
Thursday • Jeudi • Jueves

Cakes & Sugarcraft magazine, issue 116, on sale

Wedding Cakes – A Design Source magazine, issue 42, on sale

27
Friday • Vendredi • Viernes

Don't forget to order Squires Kitchen Exhibition tickets. Earlybird discount ends soon!

Holocaust Memorial Day

28
Saturday • Samedi • Sábado

29
Sunday • Dimanche • Domingo

Notes

January

S	M	T	W	T	F	S
1	2	3	4	5	6	7
8	9	10	11	12	13	14
15	16	17	18	19	20	21
22	23	24	25	26	27	28
29	30	31				

février • febrero

february

heart macaroons

edibles

250g packet SK Macaroon Mix

SK Rose Professional Dust Food Colour

Buttercream

equipment

Electric mixer

2 baking trays

Non-stick baking liner

Savoy piping bag

Plain piping nozzle

1 Preheat the oven to 130°C/260°F/gas mark ½. Stack two baking trays on top of one other and line with a non-stick liner.

2 Add a little Rose dust food colour to the SK Macaroon Mix and mix it according to the instructions on the packet.

3 Place the mixture into a large savoy piping bag fitted with a plain nozzle. Pipe hearts on the baking tray, half curving to the right and half to the left.

4 Bake for 15-20 minutes. Cool on the baking tray then sandwich two halves together with buttercream.

Ann Skipp

30
Monday • Lundi • Lunes

31
Tuesday • Mardi • Martes

1
Wednesday • Mercredi • Miércoles

2
Thursday • Jeudi • Jueves

3
Friday • Vendredi • Viernes

4
Saturday • Samedi • Sábado

5
Sunday • Dimanche • Domingo

Notes

February

S	M	T	W	T	F	S
			1	2	3	4
5	6	7	8	9	10	11
12	13	14	15	16	17	18
19	20	21	22	23	24	25
26	27	28	29			

6
Monday • Lundi • Lunes

60th Anniversary of Accession of
Queen Elizabeth II

7
Tuesday • Mardi • Martes

8
Wednesday • Mercredi
• Miércoles

9
Thursday • Jeudi • Jueves

10
Friday • Vendredi • Viernes

11
Saturday • Samedi • Sábado

12
Sunday • Dimanche
• Domingo

Notes

13
Monday • Lundi • Lunes

14
Tuesday • Mardi • Martes

15
Wednesday • Mercredi • Miércoles

16
Thursday • Jeudi • Jueves

St. Valentine's Day

17
Friday • Vendredi • Viernes

18
Saturday • Samedi • Sábado

19
Sunday • Dimanche • Domingo

Notes

			February			
S	M	T	W	T	F	S
			1	2	3	4
5	6	7	8	9	10	11
12	13	14	15	16	17	18
19	20	21	22	23	24	25
26	27	28	29			

20
Monday • Lundi • Lunes

21
Tuesday • Mardi • Martes

Shrove Tuesday

22
Wednesday • Mercredi • Miércoles

Ash Wednesday

23
Thursday • Jeudi • Jueves

24
Friday • Vendredi • Viernes

25
Saturday • Samedi • Sábado

26
Sunday • Dimanche • Domingo

Notes

February

S	M	T	W	T	F	S
			1	2	3	4
5	6	7	8	9	10	11
12	13	14	15	16	17	18
19	20	21	22	23	24	25
26	27	28	29			

mars • marzo

march

bonnet biscuits

edibles

200g (7oz) plain flour

2tsp mixed spice

¼tsp salt

30g (1oz) semolina

115g (4oz) butter

115g (4oz) caster sugar

1 beaten egg

Jam

Sugarpaste in your chosen colours

equipment

Mixing bowl

Greaseproof paper

Round fluted cookie cutter

Small flower cutters and moulds

1 Sift the flour, mixed spice and salt into a mixing bowl then mix in the semolina. Lightly rub in the butter until the mixture resembles breadcrumbs then add the sugar. Add the egg and bind the mixture together to form a stiff dough.

2 Wrap the dough in greaseproof paper and place in the refrigerator for at least an hour, preferably overnight.

3 Preheat the oven to 190°C/375°F/gas mark 5. Roll out the cookie dough thinly on a lightly floured board and cut out circles using a fluted cutter. Place on a lightly greased baking tray.

4 Bake for 8-10 minutes until pale golden in colour (this time will vary depending on the size of the biscuits). Remove from the oven and leave on the tray to start to firm then place on a wire rack to cool completely.

5 To decorate the cookies, start by brushing the top with a little jam. Make a small mound of sugarpaste and secure this to the centre, then roll out some more paste and stick to the cookie to make a hat shape. Decorate with sugar ribbon and flowers in your favourite colours.

Ann Skipp

27
Monday • Lundi • Lunes

28
Tuesday • Mardi • Martes

29
Wednesday • Mercredi • Miércoles

1
Thursday • Jeudi • Jueves

St. David's Day

2
Friday • Vendredi • Viernes

3
Saturday • Samedi • Sábado

4
Sunday • Dimanche • Domingo

Notes

March

S	M	T	W	T	F	S
				1	2	3
4	5	6	7	8	9	10
11	12	13	14	15	16	17
18	19	20	21	22	23	24
25	26	27	28	29	30	31

March • Mars • Marzo

5
Monday • Lundi • Lunes

6
Tuesday • Mardi • Martes

7
Wednesday • Mercredi
• Miércoles

8
Thursday • Jeudi • Jueves

Squires Kitchen's International 4 Day School

9
Friday • Vendredi • Viernes

10
Saturday • Samedi • Sábado

11
Sunday • Dimanche
• Domingo

Notes

Squires Kitchen's 26th Annual Exhibition, Farnham

12
Monday • Lundi • Lunes

....
....
....
....
....
....
....
....
....
....
....
....
....
....
....

Commonwealth Day

Squires Kitchen's International 5 Day School

13
Tuesday • Mardi • Martes

....
....
....
....
....
....
....
....
....
....
....
....
....
....
....

14
Wednesday • Mercredi • Miércoles

....
....
....
....
....
....
....
....
....
....
....
....
....
....

15
Thursday • Jeudi • Jueves

....
....
....
....
....
....
....
....
....
....
....
....
....
....
....

16
Friday • Vendredi • Viernes

....
....
....
....
....
....
....
....
....
....
....
....
....
....

Squires Kitchen's International
5 Day School

17
Saturday • Samedi • Sábado

....
....
....
....
....
....
....
....
....
....
....
....
....
....

St. Patrick's Day

18
Sunday • Dimanche • Domingo

....
....
....
....
....
....
....
....
....
....
....
....
....

Mothering Sunday

Notes

....
....
....
....
....
....
....
....
....
....
....

March						
S	M	T	W	T	F	S
				1	2	3
4	5	6	7	8	9	10
11	12	13	14	15	16	17
18	19	20	21	22	23	24
25	26	27	28	29	30	31

March • Mars • Marzo

19
Monday • Lundi • Lunes

Bank Holiday (Northern Ireland)
Holiday (Republic of Ireland)

20
Tuesday • Mardi • Martes

21
Wednesday • Mercredi
• Miércoles

Country Living Magazine Spring Fair

22
Thursday • Jeudi • Jueves

23
Friday • Vendredi • Viernes

24
Saturday • Samedi • Sábado

25
Sunday • Dimanche
• Domingo

British Summer Time begins

Notes

Country Living Magazine Spring Fair

26
Monday • Lundi • Lunes

27
Tuesday • Mardi • Martes

28
Wednesday • Mercredi
• Miércoles

29
Thursday • Jeudi • Jueves

30
Friday • Vendredi • Viernes

31
Saturday • Samedi • Sábado

1
Sunday • Dimanche
• Domingo

Palm Sunday

Notes

April

S	M	T	W	T	F	S
1	2	3	4	5	6	7
8	9	10	11	12	13	14
15	16	17	18	19	20	21
22	23	24	25	26	27	28
29	30					

Simnel cake

edibles

Cake mixture:

175g (6oz) margarine or butter

175g (6oz) light brown sugar

3 eggs

175g (6oz) self-raising flour

175g (6oz) sultanas

75g (2½oz) currants

50g (2oz) glacé cherries

50g (2oz) mixed peel

2tsp mixed spice

A little milk (if necessary)

Other ingredients:

500g (1lb 2oz) SK Marzipan

Apricot jam

1 egg white, lightly beaten

equipment

18cm (7") round cake tin

Large mixing bowl

Rolling pin

Crimper

Easter chicks and ribbon for decoration

1 Grease and line the cake tin. Preheat the oven to 150°C/300°F/gas mark 2.

2 Mix all of the cake mixture ingredients together in a bowl.

3 Roll out third of the marzipan. Cut out an 18cm (7") circle using the cake tin as a guide.

4 Place half the cake mixture in the tin. Place the circle of marzipan on top of the mixture, then pour the remaining mixture into the tin. Bake in the oven for approximately 2½ hours or until golden brown and firm to the touch. Allow to cool completely.

5 Cut out another 18cm (7") circle of marzipan, brush the top of the cake with apricot jam and place the marzipan on the top of the cake. Crimp the edges.

6 Make 11 or 12 small marzipan balls. Brush the top of the cake with the lightly beaten egg white. Arrange the balls around the edge of the cake and brush with egg white. Place under a hot grill to lightly brown the marzipan.

7 Decorate with Easter chicks and yellow ribbon. The cake tastes even better when eaten a few days after being made.

Ann Skipp

avril • abril

april

2
Monday • Lundi • Lunes

3
Tuesday • Mardi • Martes

4
Wednesday • Mercredi
• Miércoles

5
Thursday • Jeudi • Jueves

Maundy Thursday

6
Friday • Vendredi • Viernes

7
Saturday • Samedi • Sábado

8
Sunday • Dimanche
• Domingo

Notes

Good Friday (UK)

Jewish Passover

Easter Sunday

9
Monday • Lundi • Lunes

Easter Monday (UK and Republic of Ireland)

10
Tuesday • Mardi • Martes

11
Wednesday • Mercredi • Miércoles

12
Thursday • Jeudi • Jueves

13
Friday • Vendredi • Viernes

14
Saturday • Samedi • Sábado

15
Sunday • Dimanche • Domingo

Notes

April

S	M	T	W	T	F	S
1	2	3	4	5	6	7
8	9	10	11	12	13	14
15	16	17	18	19	20	21
22	23	24	25	26	27	28
29	30					

16
Monday • Lundi • Lunes

17
Tuesday • Mardi • Martes

18
Wednesday • Mercredi
• Miércoles

19
Thursday • Jeudi • Jueves

20
Friday • Vendredi • Viernes

21
Saturday • Samedi • Sábado

22
Sunday • Dimanche
• Domingo

Notes

BSG Durham Branch Exhibition,
St. Leonard's Catholic School,
Durham

23
Monday • Lundi • Lunes

St. George's Day

24
Tuesday • Mardi • Martes

25
Wednesday • Mercredi
• Miércoles

26
Thursday • Jeudi • Jueves

Cakes & Sugarcraft magazine, issue 117, on sale

Wedding Cakes – A Design Source magazine, issue 43, on sale

27
Friday • Vendredi • Viernes

28
Saturday • Samedi • Sábado

29
Sunday • Dimanche
• Domingo

Notes

April

S	M	T	W	T	F	S
1	2	3	4	5	6	7
8	9	10	11	12	13	14
15	16	17	18	19	20	21
22	23	24	25	26	27	28
29	30					

spots and stripes macaroons

edibles

2 x 250g packets SK Macaroon Mix

SK QFC Dusts/liquids: Pink and Red

350g (12oz) strawberry buttercream made using SK Strawberry Real Fruit Fondant Icing Mix (see Recipes and Useful Information or pack instructions)

350g (12oz) raspberry buttercream (as above)

equipment

Food mixer with paddle

Spatula

Small bowl

Paper and pencil

4cm (1½") round cutter

2 baking trays

Parchment paper

Tablespoon

Small bowl

Spatula

Small paper piping bag

2 large plastic piping bags

1cm (³/₈") round piping nozzle

1 Make up two quantities of macaroon mix following the instructions on the pack. Place three large spoonfuls of the plain mix into a small bowl then colour half of the remaining mix with red food colour and the other half with pink colour.

2 Add two drops of water to the plain mix to make it a little more runny than usual and place into the paper piping bag. Snip off the tip.

3 Use the paper, pencil and round cutter to make a template for the macaroons, keeping the circles at least 1cm (³/₈") apart from each other. Place one baking tray on top of the other then place the template and parchment paper on top.

4 One at a time place the coloured macaroon mixes into the large piping bags with the nozzles and pipe the mixture onto the parchment paper following the template. As soon as you have finished piping use the uncoloured macaroon mix in the paper piping bag to pipe spots and stripes on the tops of the macaroons. You may need to cut the end of the piping bag bigger if it doesn't pipe easily.

5 Bake in a preheated oven at 130°C/250°F/ gas mark ½ for 15-20 minutes. Allow to cool before filling.

6 Make 2 flavoured buttercreams, place each one into a piping bag and pipe onto the corresponding coloured macaroons. Sandwich together in matching pairs.

Mark Tilling

30
Monday • Lundi • Lunes

1
Tuesday • Mardi • Martes

2
Wednesday • Mercredi
• Miércoles

3
Thursday • Jeudi • Jueves

4
Friday • Vendredi • Viernes

5
Saturday • Samedi • Sábado

6
Sunday • Dimanche
• Domingo

Notes

7
Monday • Lundi • Lunes

May Day Holiday (UK and Republic of Ireland)

8
Tuesday • Mardi • Martes

World Red Cross Day

9
Wednesday • Mercredi • Miércoles

10
Thursday • Jeudi • Jueves

11
Friday • Vendredi • Viernes

12
Saturday • Samedi • Sábado

13
Sunday • Dimanche • Domingo

Notes

May

S	M	T	W	T	F	S
		1	2	3	4	5
6	7	8	9	10	11	12
13	14	15	16	17	18	19
20	21	22	23	24	25	26
27	28	29	30	31		

14
Monday • Lundi • Lunes

15
Tuesday • Mardi • Martes

16
Wednesday • Mercredi • Miércoles

17
Thursday • Jeudi • Jueves

18
Friday • Vendredi • Viernes

19
Saturday • Samedi • Sábado

20
Sunday • Dimanche • Domingo

Notes

BSG 7th International Exhibition, The International Centre, Telford

Cake Design Italian Festival, Milan

21
Monday • Lundi • Lunes

22
Tuesday • Mardi • Martes

23
Wednesday • Mercredi • Miércoles

24
Thursday • Jeudi • Jueves

25
Friday • Vendredi • Viernes

26
Saturday • Samedi • Sábado

27
Sunday • Dimanche • Domingo

Notes

May

S	M	T	W	T	F	S
		1	2	3	4	5
6	7	8	9	10	11	12
13	14	15	16	17	18	19
20	21	22	23	24	25	26
27	28	29	30	31		

28
Monday • Lundi • Lunes

29
Tuesday • Mardi • Martes

30
Wednesday • Mercredi • Miércoles

31
Thursday • Jeudi • Jueves

1
Friday • Vendredi • Viernes

2
Saturday • Samedi • Sábado

3
Sunday • Dimanche • Domingo

The Queen's Diamond Jubilee

Notes

June						
S	M	T	W	T	F	S
					1	2
3	4	5	6	7	8	9
10	11	12	13	14	15	16
17	18	19	20	21	22	23
24	25	26	27	28	29	30

june

butterfly cupcakes

edibles

Cupcakes baked in Squires Kitchen Butterfly Cupcake Cases

SK Instant Mix Fondant Icing

SK Professional Liquid Food Colours: Blackberry plus colours of choice

SK Instant Mix Royal Icing

equipment

Greaseproof paper

Waxed paper

Piping bags

Piping nozzle: no. 2

Card

1 Mix the fondant icing to a pouring consistency with water following the instructions on the packet. Divide into separate bowls and colour with the liquid food colours of your choice.

2 Draw a butterfly onto greaseproof paper as a template, place onto a flat surface and secure it with a little tape or dots of royal icing.

3 Place a piece of waxed paper over the template and secure it so the paper is completely flat.

4 Mix the royal icing to soft-peak consistency according to the instructions on the packet. Put a small amount in another bowl and add Blackberry liquid food colour. Keep the bowls covered with a clean, damp cloth when not in use to prevent the icing from drying out.

5 Snip the end off a piping bag and fit it with a no. 2 nozzle. ²/₃ fill the bag with black royal icing and pipe around the butterfly outline, making sure that there are no gaps. Allow to dry slightly.

6 To prepare some coloured icing for the wings, add a little cold, pre-boiled water to some white royal icing to create a soft dropping consistency. Colour with the liquid food colours of your choice.

7 Place some coloured icing in a piping bag without a nozzle and snip off the tip with scissors. 'Flood' the top of the wings so that the icing has a cushioned effect. Allow to dry for about 10 minutes.

8 Fill the bottom of the wings in the same way. Allow the wings to dry either in a warm place, or under the heat of a lamp.

9 Pipe dots of colour onto the wings and allow to dry.

10 When completely dry, the butterflies are ready to assemble. Fold a piece of card into a wide 'M' shape. Fold a piece of waxed paper into a 'V' and place it in the valley of the card. Pipe a butterfly head and body in black royal icing onto the fold of the waxed paper. Carefully remove the wings from the paper they were piped onto and place them into the newly-piped body. Allow to dry completely before removing the sugar butterfly from the paper and card support.

11 Place the butterflies onto the prepared cupcakes. Pipe a little royal icing underneath each body to hold it in place.

Ann Skipp

4
Monday • Lundi • Lunes

5
Tuesday • Mardi • Martes

6
Wednesday • Mercredi • Miércoles

7
Thursday • Jeudi • Jueves

Holiday (Republic of Ireland)

The Queen's Diamond Jubilee

8
Friday • Vendredi • Viernes

9
Saturday • Samedi • Sábado

10
Sunday • Dimanche • Domingo

Notes

			June			
S	M	T	W	T	F	S
					1	2
3	4	5	6	7	8	9
10	11	12	13	14	15	16
17	18	19	20	21	22	23
24	25	26	27	28	29	30

11
Monday • Lundi • Lunes

12
Tuesday • Mardi • Martes

13
Wednesday • Mercredi
• Miércoles

14
Thursday • Jeudi • Jueves

BBC Good Food Show Summer, NEC Birmingham

15
Friday • Vendredi • Viernes

16
Saturday • Samedi • Sábado

17
Sunday • Dimanche
• Domingo

Notes

BBC Good Food Show Summer, NEC Birmingham

Father's Day

18
Monday • Lundi • Lunes

19
Tuesday • Mardi • Martes

20
Wednesday • Mercredi • Miércoles

21
Thursday • Jeudi • Jueves

Longest Day

22
Friday • Vendredi • Viernes

23
Saturday • Samedi • Sábado

24
Sunday • Dimanche • Domingo

Notes

June

S	M	T	W	T	F	S
					1	2
3	4	5	6	7	8	9
10	11	12	13	14	15	16
17	18	19	20	21	22	23
24	25	26	27	28	29	30

25
Monday • Lundi • Lunes

26
Tuesday • Mardi • Martes

27
Wednesday • Mercredi
• Miércoles

28
Thursday • Jeudi • Jueves

29
Friday • Vendredi • Viernes

30
Saturday • Samedi • Sábado

1
Sunday • Dimanche
• Domingo

Armed Forces Day

Notes

July

S	M	T	W	T	F	S
1	2	3	4	5	6	7
8	9	10	11	12	13	14
15	16	17	18	19	20	21
22	23	24	25	26	27	28
29	30	31				

july

juillet • julio

butterfly biscuits

edibles

Biscuit dough (choose your
own recipe or see Recipes
and Useful Information
pages)

Sugarpaste in pastel
colours of your choice

SK Instant Mix Royal Icing

equipment

Butterfly cutter

Small circle cutters

Rolling pin

Piping bags

Piping nozzle: no. 1

Scissors

Decorative ribbon

Cellophane bags

1 Prepare some biscuit dough according to
your favourite recipe. Use a butterfly cutter
to cut out the biscuits and cut tiny circles
from the wings. Bake and allow to cool
before decorating.

2 Make up the royal icing according to the
pack instructions. Roll out some sugarpaste
in your chosen colour to a thickness of
approximately 2mm ($^1/_8$"). Using the same
butterfly and circle cutters as before, cut out
the same shapes and stick on top of the
cookies with a little royal icing.

3 Half-fill a piping bag fitted with a no. 1
nozzle with white royal icing. Pipe the body
of the butterfly first then the outline of the
wings. Finish by adding extra decoration
to the wings, keeping both sides the same.
Allow to dry.

4 Store the biscuits in an airtight tin for up
to two weeks. When you are ready to eat
them, hang them from a table centrepiece
with ribbon or place into cellophane bags
tied with ribbon. These make ideal favours
for a summer wedding.

Ann Skipp

2
Monday • Lundi • Lunes

3
Tuesday • Mardi • Martes

4
Wednesday • Mercredi • Miércoles

5
Thursday • Jeudi • Jueves

6
Friday • Vendredi • Viernes

7
Saturday • Samedi • Sábado

8
Sunday • Dimanche • Domingo

Notes

July

S	M	T	W	T	F	S
1	2	3	4	5	6	7
8	9	10	11	12	13	14
15	16	17	18	19	20	21
22	23	24	25	26	27	28
29	30	31				

9
Monday • Lundi • Lunes

10
Tuesday • Mardi • Martes

11
Wednesday • Mercredi • Miércoles

12
Thursday • Jeudi • Jueves

Holiday (Northern Ireland)

13
Friday • Vendredi • Viernes

14
Saturday • Samedi • Sábado

15
Sunday • Dimanche • Domingo

Notes

16
Monday • Lundi • Lunes

17
Tuesday • Mardi • Martes

18
Wednesday • Mercredi
• Miércoles

19
Thursday • Jeudi • Jueves

20
Friday • Vendredi • Viernes

21
Saturday • Samedi • Sábado

22
Sunday • Dimanche
• Domingo

Notes

July

S	M	T	W	T	F	S
1	2	3	4	5	6	7
8	9	10	11	12	13	14
15	16	17	18	19	20	21
22	23	24	25	26	27	28
29	30	31				

23
Monday • Lundi • Lunes

24
Tuesday • Mardi • Martes

25
Wednesday • Mercredi
• Miércoles

26
Thursday • Jeudi • Jueves

Cakes & Sugarcraft magazine, issue 118, on sale

Wedding Cakes – A Design Source magazine, issue 44, on sale

27
Friday • Vendredi • Viernes

London 2012 Olympic Games start

28
Saturday • Samedi • Sábado

29
Sunday • Dimanche
• Domingo

Notes

July

S	M	T	W	T	F	S
1	2	3	4	5	6	7
8	9	10	11	12	13	14
15	16	17	18	19	20	21
22	23	24	25	26	27	28
29	30	31				

août • agosto

august

mr and mrs cake pops

edibles

125g (4½oz) caster sugar

250g (8¾oz) unsalted butter

2 large eggs

100g (3½oz) flour

75g (2½oz) SK Extra Brute Cocoa Powder

200g (7oz) icing sugar

250g (8¾oz) SK Easy Melt White and Dark Chocolate Coating

equipment

18cm (7") square baking tin

Greaseproof paper

Mixer

Sieve

Blender

Lolly sticks

Piping bags

Ribbon to decorate

1 Make the cake the day before the cake pops. Preheat the oven to 170°C/340°F/gas mark 3. Line an 18cm (7") square baking tin.

2 Cream 125g (4½oz) of butter and 125g (4½oz) of caster sugar together until light and fluffy. Add the eggs one at a time until they are all combined.

3 Sieve the flour and 25g (just over ¾oz) cocoa powder together and fold them into the egg mixture.

4 Bake for 25 minutes or until a skewer inserted into the centre comes out clean. Leave to cool completely.

5 To make the buttercream place 125g (4½oz) butter, 200g (7oz) of icing sugar and 50g (1¾oz) cocoa powder in a mixer and beat until light and creamy.

6 Put the cake in a blender to turn it into cake crumbs. Fold them together with the buttercream to create a thick mixture.

7 Roll the mixture into 5cm (2") balls – you should be able to make approximately 25-30 cake pops. Push a lolly stick into each one, place on a tray and leave in the fridge to harden for 1 hour.

8 Melt the SK Easy Melt White Chocolate Coating in a bain marie, making sure it doesn't get too hot. Dip half the cake pops into the coating; it should set almost instantly. Repeat with Dark Chocolate Coating.

9 To decorate, spoon a little of the melted coating into a piping bag, snip off the very end and pipe initials and scroll decorations on the pops. Finish with a small bow tied around the top of the stick.

Mark Tilling

30
Monday • Lundi • Lunes

31
Tuesday • Mardi • Martes

1
Wednesday • Mercredi • Miércoles

Tickets for Squires Kitchen's 27th Annual Exhibition go on sale this month

2
Thursday • Jeudi • Jueves

3
Friday • Vendredi • Viernes

4
Saturday • Samedi • Sábado

5
Sunday • Dimanche • Domingo

Notes

August

S	M	T	W	T	F	S
			1	2	3	4
5	6	7	8	9	10	11
12	13	14	15	16	17	18
19	20	21	22	23	24	25
26	27	28	29	30	31	

6
Monday • Lundi • Lunes

Holiday (Scotland, Republic of Ireland)

7
Tuesday • Mardi • Martes

8
Wednesday • Mercredi • Miércoles

9
Thursday • Jeudi • Jueves

10
Friday • Vendredi • Viernes

11
Saturday • Samedi • Sábado

12
Sunday • Dimanche • Domingo

Notes

13
Monday • Lundi • Lunes

14
Tuesday • Mardi • Martes

15
Wednesday • Mercredi • Miércoles

16
Thursday • Jeudi • Jueves

17
Friday • Vendredi • Viernes

18
Saturday • Samedi • Sábado

19
Sunday • Dimanche • Domingo

Notes

			August			
S	**M**	**T**	**W**	**T**	**F**	**S**
			1	2	3	4
5	6	7	8	9	10	11
12	13	14	15	16	17	18
19	20	21	22	23	24	25
26	27	28	29	30	31	

20
Monday • Lundi • Lunes

21
Tuesday • Mardi • Martes

22
Wednesday • Mercredi • Miércoles

23
Thursday • Jeudi • Jueves

24
Friday • Vendredi • Viernes

25
Saturday • Samedi • Sábado

26
Sunday • Dimanche • Domingo

Notes

27
Monday • Lundi • Lunes

Late Summer Holiday (UK)

28
Tuesday • Mardi • Martes

29
Wednesday • Mercredi • Miércoles

London 2012 Paralympic Games start

30
Thursday • Jeudi • Jueves

31
Friday • Vendredi • Viernes

1
Saturday • Samedi • Sábado

2
Sunday • Dimanche • Domingo

Notes

September

S	M	T	W	T	F	S
30						1
2	3	4	5	6	7	8
9	10	11	12	13	14	15
16	17	18	19	20	21	22
23	24	25	26	27	28	29

rose cupcakes

edibles

Selection of mini cupcakes baked in cases by Squires Kitchen and Vestli House

Butter (for buttercream)

SK Instant Mix Real Fruit Fondant Icing Mix: flavour of your choice

SK Sugar Florist Paste (SFP): Pale Green, Pale Pink

Royal icing (small amount)

SK Professional Paste Food Colour: Daffodil

SK Gildesol or white vegetable fat

equipment

Savoy piping bags

Small greaseproof piping bag

Piping nozzles: medium star, no. 1 plain

SK Great Impressions Silicone Rose Mould

Non-stick board

Small rolling pin

Small rose leaf cutter

SK Great Impressions Rose Leaf Veiner

Small flower paper punch

Small ball tool

1 Make enough buttercream to ice all of the mini cupcakes using your choice of SK Instant Mix Real Fruit Fondant Icing Mix, following the instructions on the packet.

2 Pipe the buttercream icing onto the cupcakes using a large Savoy piping bag fitted with a medium sized star nozzle.

3 To make the roses, grease the rose mould with Gildesol or white vegetable fat. Push a small ball of Pale Pink SFP into the centre of the mould, flatten the top of the paste then flex the mould to remove the rose. Make one for each cupcake.

4 Roll out some Pale Green SFP thinly on a greased board and use a cutter to cut enough leaves for your cupcakes. Vein each leaf in the veiner then bend slightly to give movement.

5 Roll out some White SFP very thinly and allow to firm for a few nimutes. Place the firmed paste into a daisy paper punch and cut out several flowers. Gently push a ball tool into the centre of each one to encourage the petals to bend upwards and leave to dry. Colour a small amount of royal icing with Daffodil paste colour, place into a piping bag fitted with a no. 1 nozzle and pipe a centre onto each flower.

6 Add the roses and leaves to the centres of the piped buttercream then add the daisies around them. Do this just before serving as buttercream icing can make decorations go a little soft.

Ann Skipp

september

September • Septembre • Septiembre

3
Monday • Lundi • Lunes

4
Tuesday • Mardi • Martes

5
Wednesday • Mercredi • Miércoles

6
Thursday • Jeudi • Jueves

Inspired by Food magazine, issue 10, on sale

7
Friday • Vendredi • Viernes

8
Saturday • Samedi • Sábado

9
Sunday • Dimanche • Domingo

Notes

2nd Squires Kitchen Exposition, Vinci Centre, Tours, France

10
Monday • Lundi • Lunes

11
Tuesday • Mardi • Martes

12
Wednesday • Mercredi • Miércoles

13
Thursday • Jeudi • Jueves

14
Friday • Vendredi • Viernes

15
Saturday • Samedi • Sábado

16
Sunday • Dimanche • Domingo

Notes

September

S	M	T	W	T	F	S
30						1
2	3	4	5	6	7	8
9	10	11	12	13	14	15
16	17	18	19	20	21	22
23	24	25	26	27	28	29

September • Septembre • Septiembre

17
Monday • Lundi • Lunes

Jewish New Year

18
Tuesday • Mardi • Martes

19
Wednesday • Mercredi
• Miércoles

20
Thursday • Jeudi • Jueves

21
Friday • Vendredi • Viernes

22
Saturday • Samedi • Sábado

Autumnal Equinox

23
Sunday • Dimanche
• Domingo

Notes

24
Monday • Lundi • Lunes

25
Tuesday • Mardi • Martes

26
Wednesday • Mercredi • Miércoles

Jewish Day of Atonement

27
Thursday • Jeudi • Jueves

28
Friday • Vendredi • Viernes

29
Saturday • Samedi • Sábado

30
Sunday • Dimanche • Domingo

Notes

September

S	M	T	W	T	F	S
30						1
2	3	4	5	6	7	8
9	10	11	12	13	14	15
16	17	18	19	20	21	22
23	24	25	26	27	28	29

mini lemon cupcakes

edibles

Cake mixture:

125g (4½oz) butter

125g (4½oz) caster sugar

2 eggs

125g (4½oz) self-raising flour

½tsp concentrated lemon juice

Medium-sized mixing bowl

Topping:

1 quantity lemon buttercream made using SK Lemon Real Fruit Fondant Icing Mix (see Recipes and Useful Information or pack instructions)

Jelly Belly lemon jelly bean

equipment

Wooden spoon or hand-held electric mixer

SK Yellow Mini Cupcake Cases

Mini muffin pan

Savoy nozzle

Piping bag

Makes 24

1 Preheat the oven to 160°C/320°F/gas mark 2.

2 Cream the butter and sugar together until light and fluffy. Add the eggs one at a time until they are all combined and mix in the lemon juice. Fold in the flour.

3 Place the SK Mini Cupcake Cases into a mini muffin pan and pipe or spoon the mixture to about halfway up the cases.

4 Bake for about 10 minutes or until golden brown on top then allow to cool on a cooling rack.

5 Make up the lemon buttercream and place into a piping bag with a Savoy nozzle. Pipe round the edge of the mini cupcake, working up to the centre. Top off with a lemon jelly bean.

Ann Skipp

october

October • Octobre • Octubre

1
Monday • Lundi • Lunes

2
Tuesday • Mardi • Martes

3
Wednesday • Mercredi
• Miércoles

4
Thursday • Jeudi • Jueves

5
Friday • Vendredi • Viernes

6
Saturday • Samedi • Sábado

7
Sunday • Dimanche
• Domingo

Notes

8
Monday • Lundi • Lunes

9
Tuesday • Mardi • Martes

10
Wednesday • Mercredi • Miércoles

11
Thursday • Jeudi • Jueves

12
Friday • Vendredi • Viernes

13
Saturday • Samedi • Sábado

14
Sunday • Dimanche • Domingo

Notes

October

S	M	T	W	T	F	S
	1	2	3	4	5	6
7	8	9	10	11	12	13
14	15	16	17	18	19	20
21	22	23	24	25	26	27
28	29	30	31			

15
Monday • Lundi • Lunes

16
Tuesday • Mardi • Martes

17
Wednesday • Mercredi • Miércoles

18
Thursday • Jeudi • Jueves

19
Friday • Vendredi • Viernes

20
Saturday • Samedi • Sábado

21
Sunday • Dimanche • Domingo

Notes

22
Monday • Lundi • Lunes

23
Tuesday • Mardi • Martes

24
Wednesday • Mercredi • Miércoles

United Nations Day

25
Thursday • Jeudi • Jueves

Cakes & Sugarcraft magazine, issue 119, on sale

Wedding Cakes – A Design Source magazine, issue 45, on sale

26
Friday • Vendredi • Viernes

27
Saturday • Samedi • Sábado

28
Sunday • Dimanche • Domingo

British Summer Time ends

BBC Good Food Show Scotland, SECC Glasgow

Notes

October

S	M	T	W	T	F	S
	1	2	3	4	5	6
7	8	9	10	11	12	13
14	15	16	17	18	19	20
21	22	23	24	25	26	27
28	29	30	31			

Week 43

29
Monday • Lundi • Lunes

Holiday (Republic of Ireland)

30
Tuesday • Mardi • Martes

31
Wednesday • Mercredi • Miércoles

Hallowe'en

1
Thursday • Jeudi • Jueves

All Saints' Day

2
Friday • Vendredi • Viernes

3
Saturday • Samedi • Sábado

4
Sunday • Dimanche • Domingo

Notes

November

S	M	T	W	T	F	S
				1	2	3
4	5	6	7	8	9	10
11	12	13	14	15	16	17
18	19	20	21	22	23	24
25	26	27	28	29	30	

novembre • noviembre

november

chocolate truffles

edibles

250g packet of SK Chocolate Ganache Mix

85ml (2¾oz) cooled, boiled water

50g (1¾oz) butter, cut into small cubes

150g (5¼oz) SK Dark Belgian Couverture Chocolate (for rolling)

150g (5¼oz) SK Extra Brute Cocoa Powder (for rolling)

1 Mix the SK Chocolate Ganache Mix with 85ml (2¾oz) of cooled, boiled water and heat in the microwave on full power for 1 minute, stirring every 20 seconds until melted.

2 While the ganache is still warm, add the butter and stir until melted. (If you find the butter is not melting, heat in a microwave for 10 seconds and stir again.)

3 Place in a container in the fridge and leave overnight until set.

4 Roll the truffle mixture into approximately 15-20 x 2.5cm (1") balls. Place on a tray and return to the fridge.

5 Wearing plastic gloves, roll the truffle in your hands, use a little melted SK Dark Belgian Couverture Chocolate to coat the outside of the truffle then roll it in cocoa powder.

Mark Tilling

5
Monday • Lundi • Lunes

Guy Fawkes Night

6
Tuesday • Mardi • Martes

7
Wednesday • Mercredi • Miércoles

8
Thursday • Jeudi • Jueves

9
Friday • Vendredi • Viernes

International Cake Show, NEC Birmingham

MasterChef Live, Olympia Exhibition Centre, London

10
Saturday • Samedi • Sábado

11
Sunday • Dimanche • Domingo

Remembrance Sunday

Notes

			November			
S	M	T	W	T	F	S
				1	2	3
4	5	6	7	8	9	10
11	12	13	14	15	16	17
18	19	20	21	22	23	24
25	26	27	28	29	30	

12
Monday • Lundi • Lunes

13
Tuesday • Mardi • Martes

14
Wednesday • Mercredi • Miércoles

15
Thursday • Jeudi • Jueves

Muslim New Year (provisional)

16
Friday • Vendredi • Viernes

17
Saturday • Samedi • Sábado

18
Sunday • Dimanche • Domingo

Notes

19
Monday • Lundi • Lunes

20
Tuesday • Mardi • Martes

21
Wednesday • Mercredi
• Miércoles

22
Thursday • Jeudi • Jueves

BBC Good Food Show Winter, NEC Birmingham

23
Friday • Vendredi • Viernes

24
Saturday • Samedi • Sábado

25
Sunday • Dimanche
• Domingo

Notes

BBC Good Food Show Winter, NEC Birmingham

November

S	M	T	W	T	F	S
				1	2	3
4	5	6	7	8	9	10
11	12	13	14	15	16	17
18	19	20	21	22	23	24
25	26	27	28	29	30	

26
Monday • Lundi • Lunes

27
Tuesday • Mardi • Martes

28
Wednesday • Mercredi • Miércoles

29
Thursday • Jeudi • Jueves

30
Friday • Vendredi • Viernes

St. Andrew's Day

1
Saturday • Samedi • Sábado

2
Sunday • Dimanche • Domingo

First Sunday of Advent

Notes

December						
S	M	T	W	T	F	S
30	31					1
2	3	4	5	6	7	8
9	10	11	12	13	14	15
16	17	18	19	20	21	22
23	24	25	26	27	28	29

décembre • diciembre

december

christmas pudding whoopie pies

edibles

Pies:

115g (4oz) butter

200g (7oz) caster sugar

1 large egg

225ml (8fl oz) milk

280g (9¾oz) plain flour

50g (1¾oz) SK Extra Brute Cocoa Powder

2½tsp bicarbonate of soda

Filling:

50ml (1¾fl oz) milk

100g (3½oz) white marshmallows

½ vanilla pod

100g (3½oz) icing sugar

115g (4oz) unsalted butter

Topping:

100g (3½oz) SK White Belgian Chocolate

SK Sugar Dough: Green and Red

PME holly leaf plunger cutter: small

equipment

Baking tray

Baking paper

Mixer

Sieve

Piping bags

Saucepan

Non-stick board

Small rolling pin

1 Preheat the oven to 170°C/340°F/gas mark 3 and line a baking tray with baking paper.

2 Cream the butter and sugar together until light and fluffy. Mix in the egg. Add the milk slowly and keep mixing until fully incorporated.

3 Sieve the flour with the cocoa powder and bicarbonate of soda then fold it into the mix.

4 Put the mix in a piping bag, snip off the end and pipe into approximately 12-15 x 4cm (1½") discs.

5 Bake in the oven for 10-15 minutes or until firm. Allow to cool.

6 To make the filling, heat the milk in a saucepan. Stir in the marshmallows until they have melted. Remove from the heat, stir in the vanilla pod seeds and allow to cool.

7 Cream the butter and sugar together in a mixer with a paddle. Add the cooled marshmallow mixture and mix until it reaches a light and fluffy consistency. Spoon or pipe onto one half of a whoopie pie and sandwich with another half.

8 Melt and temper the white chocolate. Pour a little on top of each whoopie to look like custard. Allow to set.

9 Roll out the Green Sugar Dough to about 2mm (⅛") thick. Cut out two holly leaves for each macaroon using the mini cutter. Roll three small balls of Red Sugar Dough for each macaroon. Put some melted white chocolate in a piping bag and use it to stick the leaves and berries on top of the whoopie pies.

Mark Tilling

3
Monday • Lundi • Lunes

4
Tuesday • Mardi • Martes

5
Wednesday • Mercredi • Miércoles

Last posting date for Christmas, International Airmail: countries outside Europe, USA and Canada

6
Thursday • Jeudi • Jueves

7
Friday • Vendredi • Viernes

8
Saturday • Samedi • Sábado

9
Sunday • Dimanche • Domingo

Notes

December

S	M	T	W	T	F	S
30	31					1
2	3	4	5	6	7	8
9	10	11	12	13	14	15
16	17	18	19	20	21	22
23	24	25	26	27	28	29

10
Monday • Lundi • Lunes

Last posting date for Christmas,
International Airmail: Eastern
Europe, USA and Canada

11
Tuesday • Mardi • Martes

12
Wednesday • Mercredi
• Miércoles

Last posting date for Christmas,
International Airmail: Western
Europe

13
Thursday • Jeudi • Jueves

14
Friday • Vendredi • Viernes

Last posting date for Christmas,
Standard Parcels

15
Saturday • Samedi • Sábado

16
Sunday • Dimanche
• Domingo

Notes

17
Monday • Lundi • Lunes

18
Tuesday • Mardi • Martes

*Last posting date for Christmas,
Second Class*

19
Wednesday • Mercredi
• Miércoles

20
Thursday • Jeudi • Jueves

*Last posting date for Christmas,
first Class*

21
Friday • Vendredi • Viernes

22
Saturday • Samedi • Sábado

*Last courier date from squires-shop.
com for Christmas*

23
Sunday • Dimanche
• Domingo

Shortest Day

Notes

December

S	M	T	W	T	F	S
30	31					1
2	3	4	5	6	7	8
9	10	11	12	13	14	15
16	17	18	19	20	21	22
23	24	25	26	27	28	29

24
Monday • Lundi • Lunes

25
Tuesday • Mardi • Martes

26
Wednesday • Mercredi • Miércoles

27
Thursday • Jeudi • Jueves

Boxing Day (UK); Holiday (UK and Republic of Ireland)

Christmas Day; Holiday (UK and Republic of Ireland)

St. Stephen's Day (Republic of Ireland)

28
Friday • Vendredi • Viernes

29
Saturday • Samedi • Sábado

30
Sunday • Dimanche • Domingo

Notes

31
Monday • Lundi • Lunes

1
Tuesday • Mardi • Martes

New Year's Day

2
Wednesday • Mercredi • Miércoles

3
Thursday • Jeudi • Jueves

4
Friday • Vendredi • Viernes

5
Saturday • Samedi • Sábado

6
Sunday • Dimanche • Domingo

Notes

January 2013

S	M	T	W	T	F	S
		1	2	3	4	5
6	7	8	9	10	11	12
13	14	15	16	17	18	19
20	21	22	23	24	25	26
27	28	29	30	31		

	January	February	March	April	May	June
1						
2						
3						
4						
5						
6						
7						
8						
9						
10						
11						
12						
13						
14						
15						
16						
17						
18						
19						
20						
21						
22						
23						
24						
25						
26						
27						
28						
29						
30						
31						

July	August	September	October	November	December	
						1
						2
						3
						4
						5
						6
						7
						8
						9
						10
						11
						12
						13
						14
						15
						16
						17
						18
						19
						20
						21
						22
						23
						24
						25
						26
						27
						28
						29
						30
						31

recipes and useful information

vanilla sponge

1 Beat the butter and sugar together until fluffy and light in colour.

2 Beat the eggs, then add them to the mixture a little at a time, beating in thoroughly before adding more. If the mixture looks like it is splitting, add in a tablespoon of the flour.

3 Fold in the flour using a metal spoon.

4 Add the vanilla essence.

5 Transfer the mixture to the prepared baking tin, making sure that it is slightly lower in the centre.

6 Bake in a preheated oven at 180°C/350°F/gas mark 4, until the cake is a golden brown colour and springy to the touch.

Variation: lemon cake

- Substitute the vanilla in the recipe for concentrated lemon juice.

- When making the buttercream, add 10-20ml (½-¾fl oz) of lemon juice.

Variation: simple chocolate cake

- Add 25g (1oz) of cocoa for every 225g (8oz) of flour and 15ml (1tbsp) of milk for each 25g (1oz) of cocoa to ensure that the mixture is not too dry.

Helen Penman

Square	12.5cm (5")	15cm (6")	17.5cm (7")	20.5cm (8")	23cm (9")	25.5cm (10")	28cm (11")
Round	15cm (6")	17.5cm (7")	20.5cm (8")	23cm (9")	25.5cm (10")	28cm (11")	30.5cm (12")
Softened butter	175g (6oz)	260g (9oz)	430g (15oz)	510g (1lb 2oz)	690g (1lb 8oz)	770g (1lb 11oz)	940g (2lb 1oz)
Caster sugar	175g (6oz)	260g (9oz)	430g (15oz)	510g (1lb 2oz)	690g (1lb 8oz)	770g (1lb 11oz)	940g (2lb 1oz)
Eggs (medium)	3	4	7	8	10	11	13
Self-raising flour	225g (8oz)	340g (12oz)	560g (1lb 4oz)	700g (1lb 8oz)	1kg (2lb 3oz)	1.14kg (2lb 8oz)	1.3kg (2lb 14oz)
Vanilla essence	½tsp	1tsp	2½tsp	3tsp	4tsp	4½tsp	5½tsp
Baking times	¾-1 hour	1-1 hour 10 minutes	1¼-1 hour 20 minutes	1½-1 hours 40 minutes	1¾-2 hours	2¼-2½ hours	2½-2¾ hours

chocolate sponge

1 Sift all the dry ingredients into a bowl.

2 Beat the butter and sugar together until light and fluffy in texture.

3 Beat the eggs and add to the butter mixture a little at a time. If the mixture looks like it is going to split, add a tablespoon of the dry ingredients, then continue adding the egg.

4 Add the vanilla essence and beat well. Add the sour cream and mix gently.

5 Fold the dry ingredients into the mixture using a metal spoon. Only add the water if the mixture is too stiff.

6 Carefully spoon the mixture into the prepared cake tin and bake in the centre of the oven for the suggested time at 190°C/370°F/gas mark 5.

Variation: chocolate and cherry cake

- Add 90g (3oz) of dried or glacé cherries to the basic recipe.

Helen Penman

Square	12.5cm (5")	15cm (6")	17.5cm (7")	20.5cm (8")	23cm (9")	25.5cm (10")	28cm (11")	30.5cm (12")
Round	15cm (6")	17.5cm (7")	20.5cm (8")	23cm (9")	25.5cm (10")	28cm (11")	30.5cm (12")	(33cm) (13")
Softened butter	85g (2¾oz)	115g (4oz)	150g (5¼oz)	225g (8oz)	310g (10¾oz)	340g (12oz)	425g (14¾oz)	510g (1lb 2oz)
Soft brown sugar	195g (6¾oz)	285g (10oz)	450g (1lb)	560g (1lb 4oz)	720g (1lb 10oz)	860g (1lb 14oz)	1kg (2lb 3oz)	1.25kg (2lb 12oz)
Cocoa powder	20g (¾oz)	30g (1oz)	50g (1¾oz)	60g (2oz)	80g (2½oz)	90g (3oz)	110g (3¾oz)	120g (4¼oz)
Water	60ml (2fl oz)	90ml (3fl oz)	145ml (5fl oz)	175ml (6fl oz)	225ml (8fl oz)	260ml (9fl oz)	315ml (11fl oz)	370ml (13fl oz)
Plain flour	150g (5¼oz)	225g (8oz)	375g (13¼oz)	450g (1lb)	750g (1lb 10oz)	800g (1lb 12oz)	1.1kg (2lb 6oz)	1.35kg (3lb)
Baking powder	1¼tsp	2tsp	2½tsp	4tsp	4tsp	6tsp	7¼tsp	8½tsp
Bicarbonate of soda + salt	⅓tsp	½tsp	1¼tsp	2tsp	3tsp	3¾tsp	4tsp	4¼tsp
Vanilla essence	1tsp	1tsp	1¼tsp	2tsp	3tsp	3¾tsp	4tsp	4¼tsp
Eggs (large)	2	2	3	4	5	6	7	8
Sour cream	75ml (2½fl oz)	150ml (5fl oz)	200ml (7fl oz)	300ml (10½fl oz)	335ml (11¾fl oz)	450ml (15½fl oz)	540ml (19½fl oz)	580ml (1pt)
Baking times	¾-1 hour	1-1 hour 10 minutes	1¼ -1 hour 20 minutes	1½-1 hours 40 minutes	1¾-2 hours	2¼-2½ hours	2½-2¾ hours	2¾-3 hours

fillings

Sugar syrup

Brushing sugar syrup onto a sponge cake will help to keep it moist. Adding flavouring to the syrup is optional – seedless jams work well. The amount of syrup you use will depend on your own preference – the more you use the sweeter and moister the cake will be.

You will need:

115g (4oz) caster sugar

125ml (4½fl oz) water

5ml (1tsp) flavouring (optional)

Makes 240ml (8½fl oz)

1 Put the caster sugar and water into a saucepan and flavouring (if required) on a low heat. Slowly bring to the boil, stirring constantly to prevent the sugar from burning. Simmer for one minute to ensure all the sugar granules have dissolved completely. Remove from the heat and set aside to cool.

2 Store in an airtight container and refrigerate. Use within one month.

Ganache

Ganache is a perfect filling for chocolate cakes. This standard recipe will cover a 15cm and 20cm (6" and 8") stacked cake, round or square.

You will need:

Milk and white chocolate:

> 400g (14¼oz) chocolate
>
> 300ml (10½fl oz) whipping cream

Dark chocolate:

> 400g (14¼oz) chocolate
>
> 350ml (12¼fl oz) whipping cream

If you are adding a 25cm (10") cake double the standard recipe.

If you are adding a 30cm (12") cake multiply the recipe by 2.5.

1 Heat the whipping cream and pour on to the couverture chocolate and leave for 5 minutes. After this time, carefully start to stir the mixture with a balloon whisk. Do not whisk, as you will get air bubbles in the ganache. The chocolate and cream should combine easily.

2 Leave the ganache to cool and harden then store in the fridge until required. If it is too stiff to spread, gently warm it in a double boiler (bain marie) to bring it to spreading consistency.

Buttercream

This recipe makes enough to fill and cover a 28cm (11") round cake.

You will need:

225g (8oz) butter, softened

1kg (2lb 3¼oz) icing sugar

15-30ml (1-2tbsp) syrup (vanilla or a flavour of your choice to complement the cake) or fresh fruit juice

Makes approximately 1.2kg (2lb 11oz)

1 Beat the butter and add the icing sugar in small amounts until it is all incorporated and the mixture is smooth.

2 Add the syrup/flavouring a little at a time until the buttercream has a soft consistency; add more if a softer texture is needed (you might find this when crumb-coating the surface of cakes as a softer icing won't pull the cake into crumbs).

Fruity buttercream

This alternative to buttercream is very simple to make and is perfect for topping cupcakes. Choose a fruit flavour to complement your cake.

You will need:

250g (8¾oz) pack SK Real Fruit Fondant Icing Mix in your choice of flavour

125g (4½oz) butter, softened

A few drops of cooled, boiled water

Makes 375g (13¼oz)

1 Place the fondant and butter into a bowl and add a few drops of cooled, boiled water to soften the mixture.

2 Beat the ingredients together until light and fluffy.

vanilla cupcakes

You will need:

115g (4oz) margarine

115g (4oz) caster sugar

2 large eggs

Vanilla essence

115g (4oz) self-raising flour

Medium-sized mixing bowl

Wooden spoon or hand-held electric mixer

Small bowl

Fork

Sieve

Metal tablespoon

Cupcake cases

Metal muffin tin

Two teaspoons

Makes 12-15 large cupcakes

1 Preheat the oven to 180°C/350°F/ gas mark 4.

2 Allow the margarine to soften then place into the mixing bowl with the sugar, beat with a wooden spoon or (preferably) a hand-held electric mixer until the mixture is light and fluffy.

3 Beat the eggs with a fork then gradually add them to the mixture, beating constantly to prevent the mixture from curdling. Once all of the egg has been added, add the vanilla essence.

4 Sift the flour over the mixture and fold in gently with a metal spoon, making sure all of the flour is combined without knocking the air out of the mixture.

5 Place the SK Dotty cupcake cases in the muffin tin and use two teaspoons to spoon mixture into each of the cases until they are ¾ full.

6 Bake in the oven for 12-15 minutes. When the cakes are golden and firm to the touch, carefully remove from the oven and leave in the tin until cool.

mini vanilla cupcakes

You will need:

125g (4½oz) butter

125g (4½oz) caster sugar

2 eggs

125g (4½oz) self-raising flour

Medium-sized mixing bowl

Wooden spoon or hand-held electric mixer

Mini cupcake cases

Mini muffin pan

Makes 24

1 Preheat the oven to 160°C/320°F/gas mark 2.

2 Cream the butter and sugar together until light and fluffy. Add the eggs one at a time until they are all combined. Fold in the flour.

3 Place the SK Mini Cupcake Cases into a mini muffin pan and pipe or spoon the mixture to about halfway up the cases.

4 Bake for about 10 minutes or until golden brown on top then allow to cool on a cooling rack.

how to ice a cupcake

Savoy nozzle

Place a large, round nozzle into a piping bag and fill with buttercream. Start by piping around the edge of the cupcake, keeping it as close to the edge as possible.

Pipe all the way round and finish with a small rosette in the centre.

Start again on top of the first round of piped fondant.

Finish with a small rosette on top. Your cupcake is now ready to decorate!

Palette knife

Place a large amount of buttercream icing on top of the cupcake with a palette knife.

Use the knife to work the buttercream down to the sides of the case. Hold the palette knife at a 45° angle to the top of the cupcake.

Move the knife around the cake to make the icing peak.

Push down into the centre of the icing and drag the knife in a clockwise direction around the top to make a swirl effect.

easy cake pops

You will need:

400g (14oz) baked sponge cake (any type is fine)

100g (3½oz) vanilla buttercream

Lolly sticks

SK White, Milk or Dark Belgian Chocolate

SK Coloured Vermicelli

Small volcano silicone mould (optional)

Silicone paper

1 Break the cake up into crumbs, add the buttercream and mix well until combined.

2 Spoon the mix into the volcano-shaped moulds, compressing and levelling the mixture with the top of the mould. Alternatively, roll balls of paste between your hands. Insert a lolly stick into the middle of each one and refrigerate for 15 minutes.

3 Temper the chocolate. Remove the cake pops from the fridge, dip into the chocolate then dip into the chocolate vermicelli, sugar sprinkles or other decoration of your choice.

4 Lay on a sheet of silicone paper and leave to set.

biscuits

You will need:

175g (6oz) butter

55g (2oz) caster sugar

225g (8oz) self-raising flour, sifted

Cookie cutters

Baking trays, lightly greased

Wire cooling rack

1 Preheat the oven to 180°C/350°F/gas mark 4.

2 Cream the butter and the caster sugar together until light and creamy. Gradually add the sifted self-raising flour, then knead together lightly.

3 Roll out the dough to a thickness of 5mm (¼") and cut out the shapes you require using cookie cutters. Place on the greased baking trays and bake for 8-10 minutes until pale brown. Leave to cool on a wire rack.

whoopie pies

You will need:

75g (2½oz) unsalted butter

1 egg

150g (5¼oz) caster sugar

125g (4½oz) soured cream

25ml (just over ¾fl oz) cold milk

1tsp vanilla extract

55g (2oz) SK White Belgian Chocolate, roughly chopped

¾tsp bicarbonate of soda

275g (9¾oz) plain flour

Savoy piping nozzle

Piping bag

For the filling:

100g (3½oz) mini white marshmallows

50ml (1¾oz) milk

125g (4½oz) softened unsalted butter

For the decoration:

Bowl of SK White Chocolate, tempered

SK Coloured Vermicelli

Makes 20

1 Preheat the oven to 180°C/350°F/gas mark 4. Line a baking tray with non-stick parchment paper.

2 Gently melt the butter and leave to one side. Whisk the egg until light and fluffy. Beat in the caster sugar ⅓ at a time until thick.

3 Beat the melted butter, soured cream, milk, vanilla and chopped SK White Belgian Chocolate into the egg and sugar mixture. Sift the bicarbonate of soda and plain flour into the mixture and beat until well combined.

4 Place the mixture into a piping bag fitted with a savoy nozzle and pipe onto the parchment paper into balls approximately 2.5cm (1") in diameter. Make sure they are well spaced to allow for spreading during baking.

5 Bake the cakes in the oven for 13-14 minutes until lightly golden and firm to touch. Place the cakes on a cooling rack and allow to cool completely.

Filling

1 Heat the mini white marshmallows and milk in a small saucepan over a gentle heat, stirring constantly until smooth. Allow the mixture to cool.

2 Beat the butter until fluffy and light in colour then gradually beat into the marshmallow mixture until smooth.

3 Spoon the filling into a piping bag fitted with a savoy nozzle. Pipe the filling onto one half of a whoopie pie then sandwich a second half on top. Press the two halves together lightly to bring the filling to the edge of the cake.

4 Dip half of a whoopie pie side-on into the tempered white chocolate and remove any surplus chocolate on the edge of the bowl.

5 Dip the chocolate-coated area into the SK Coloured Vermicelli in the colour of your choice and refrigerate the pies until set.

tempering chocolate

What is tempering?

Chocolate should be tempered before being used in moulds or to coat cakes or pralines. In short, whenever the chocolate needs to be hard and glossy once set.

If chocolate is melted in the normal way then left to cool, the finished product is usually grainy, dull and stays quite soft.

The main ingredient of chocolate is cocoa butter, so the purpose of tempering chocolate is to 'precrystallise' the cocoa butter in the chocolate, or to change it into a stable crystalline form. This ensures the hardness, shrinking force and gloss of the finished product after it has cooled. This is achieved by bringing chocolate up to the right working temperature so that there are sufficient stable crystals. The three factors which are important during tempering are time, temperature and movement.

PLEASE NOTE: When you add chocolate to dishes to add flavour, such as when preparing mousses, you can usually melt the chocolate without tempering.

Tempering in the microwave

1 Place the chocolate pieces in a plastic or glass bowl.

2 Put the bowl into the microwave and melt the chocolate at 800-1000W.

3 Take the chocolate out of the microwave every 15 to 20 seconds and stir well to ensure that the temperature of the chocolate is evenly distributed and that it does not scorch.

4 Repeat this procedure until the chocolate has almost all melted. Some small pieces of chocolate should still be visible in the bowl.

5 Remove from the heat and stir the chocolate well, until all the pieces of chocolate have disappeared and a slightly thickened, even liquid has been obtained. The chocolate is now tempered and ready to work with.

Tips for making your own chocolates

• Temper the chocolate and pour it into a bowl. Ensure that the bowl is well filled so that the tempered chocolate remains at temperature for as long as possible without becoming overcrystallised too quickly (becoming too thick).

• If you are you working on marble or a cold plate, put a piece of cloth or something warm under the bowl of chocolate so that the temperature of the chocolate doesn't decrease too rapidly. That prevents too rapid a crystallisation.

• The closer the temperature of the filling is to the temperature of the tempered chocolate, the better the end result. Naturally this is impossible for certain fillings (e.g. buttercream fillings). In that case, ensure that the filling is not too cold but is still stiff enough to be dipped. With coatings, temperature plays a lesser role; you can even dip deep-frozen fillings.

• Once you have dipped all the chocolates, don't place them immediately into the refrigerator, but first let them set at room temperature for about a quarter of an hour. Abrupt temperature changes take off the chocolate glaze and if the chocolate layer is thin, can even break it.

guide to using chocolate transfers

1 Select your pattern. Be careful when handling the transfer, because the cocoa butter on the acetate could melt.

2 Put the transfer on a flat surface. The side that you cover with chocolate is the rougher of the two sides.

3 Pour on some tempered chocolate, enough so that when you smooth it with a palette knife the chocolate is about 1-2mm thick.

4 Completely cover the transfer then move it to a clean area of your work surface.

5 Allow the chocolate to just start to cool. Cut the chocolate into the required shapes, taking care not to cut through the acetate backing.

6 To make panels, cut into rectangles the height of the cake you are covering.

7 When the chocolate is hard, turn the acetate over onto a piece of greaseproof paper with a little weight on top in order to keep it flat.

8 Place the chocolate-covered transfers in the refrigerator for a while before peeling the acetate away from the chocolate.

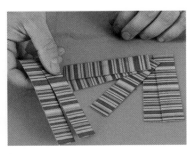

9 The panels are now ready to arrange around the side of the cake.

high quality food colours from Squires Kitchen

Squires Kitchen's colours are guaranteed edible and confirm to EU directives for use in foodstuff. All colours in the Professional and QFC Dust, Liquid and Paste ranges (excluding Pollen-style Dusts) are certified gluten-free.

SK Double Strength Professional Paste Food Colours, SK Professional Liquid Food Colours, SK Professional Dust Food Colours

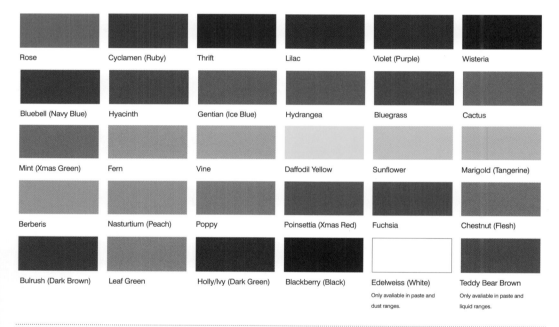

Rose	Cyclamen (Ruby)	Thrift	Lilac	Violet (Purple)	Wisteria
Bluebell (Navy Blue)	Hyacinth	Gentian (Ice Blue)	Hydrangea	Bluegrass	Cactus
Mint (Xmas Green)	Fern	Vine	Daffodil Yellow	Sunflower	Marigold (Tangerine)
Berberis	Nasturtium (Peach)	Poppy	Poinsettia (Xmas Red)	Fuchsia	Chestnut (Flesh)
Bulrush (Dark Brown)	Leaf Green	Holly/Ivy (Dark Green)	Blackberry (Black)	Edelweiss (White)	Teddy Bear Brown

Edelweiss (White): Only avaliable in paste and dust ranges.

Teddy Bear Brown: Only avaliable in paste and liquid ranges.

SK QFC Pastes & Liquids

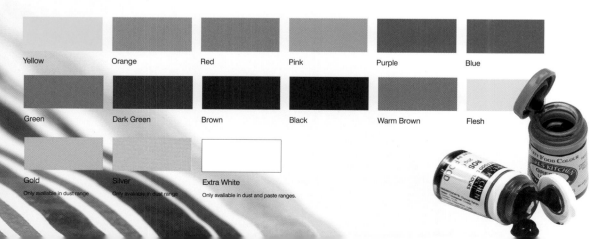

Yellow	Orange	Red	Pink	Purple	Blue
Green	Dark Green	Brown	Black	Warm Brown	Flesh
Gold	Silver	Extra White			

Gold: Only available in dust range

Silver: Only avaliable in dust range

Extra White: Only avaliable in dust and paste ranges.

SK Professional Designer Paste Food Colours

Dark Forest	Terracotta	Bordeaux	Desert Storm	Sunny Lime	Plum

Yucca	Olive	Jet	Cream

SK Professional Pastel Dust Food Colours

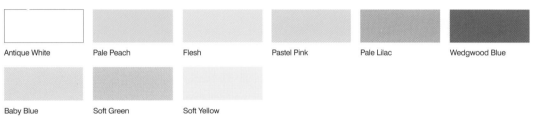

Antique White	Pale Peach	Flesh	Pastel Pink	Pale Lilac	Wedgwood Blue

Baby Blue	Soft Green	Soft Yellow

SK Professional Designer Dust Food Colours

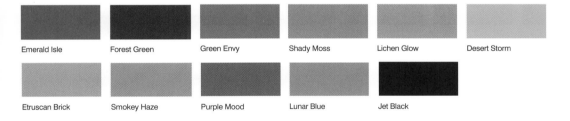

Emerald Isle	Forest Green	Green Envy	Shady Moss	Lichen Glow	Desert Storm

Etruscan Brick	Smokey Haze	Purple Mood	Lunar Blue	Jet Black

SK Professional Metallic Lustre Dust Food Colours

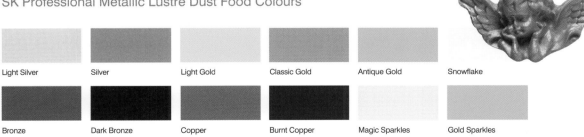

Light Silver	Silver	Light Gold	Classic Gold	Antique Gold	Snowflake

Bronze	Dark Bronze	Copper	Burnt Copper	Magic Sparkles	Gold Sparkles

SK Professional Moon Beam Dust Food Colours

Sapphire   Jade   Topaz   Ruby

SK Bridal Satin Lustre Dust Food Colours

White Satin   Alabaster   Double Cream   Delphinium   Forget-me-not   Lavender

Soft Peach   Chiffon Pink   Damask Rose   Myrtle

SK Bridal Satin Shimmer Dust Food Colours

Verona (Green)   Florence (Purple)   Roma (Peach)   Rimini (Blue)   Siena (Brown)

SK Magic Fairy Sparkle Dust Food Colours

Ice White   Primrose   Rosa   Lavender   Iris   Absinthe

SK Pollen Style Edible Dust Food Colours

Pale Yellow   Apple Green   Pale Golden   Dark Golden   Pale Green   Poppy Black

Poinsettia   Russet   Speckled   Catkin

how to use food colours

Liquid Food Colours

Suitable for use in royal icing, fondant, pastillage, buttercream, glacé icing and jellies. Liquid food colours can be used to paint directly onto sugar plaques for a clean, 'watercolour' effect (for more of a 'poster paint' colour finish use edible paints). They can also be used in an airbrush. If you're using colours for royal icing work, make sure they don't contain glucose or glycerides.

How to use

Mix in the colour a couple of drops at a time to make sure you don't add too much.

Paste Food Colours

Use paste food colours to colour white paste or to change the shade of ready-coloured pastes including sugarpaste, marzipan, flower paste, pastillage and pastry. A paintbrush can be dipped into the neat colour and used to surface paint sugar pieces to add strong definition to your work – this is particularly useful for adding markings to sugar petals and leaves.

How to use

Start by adding a tiny amount of your chosen paste food colour to the paste using a cocktail stick. Knead the colour into the paste until it is evenly blended. Repeat this process until you achieve the desired shade then leave the paste for at least half an hour sealed in a food-grade plastic bag so that the colour can mature.

Dust Food Colours

Suitable for dusting dry sugar work such as marzipan, royal icing, pastillation and sugarpaste and brilliant for enhancing the colour of realistic sugar flowers or leaves. Dust food colours can be used with or without stencils to create soft backgrounds. There are many varieties of dust food colours, for example Squires Kitchen Pollen Style Edible Dusts have been created with texture and colour in mind to give a realistic finish to your work.

How to use

Always use dust food colours sparingly. After dipping a dry, flat paintbrush into the dust, rub the bristles on a piece of kitchen towel to remove the excess colour – this will give you more control when you apply the dust to the sugar surface. If you're colouring a sugar flower or leaf, passing it through the steam from a boiling kettle will set the colour and give a slightly shiny appearance. Allow to dry.

helpful charts

Oven temperatures

Temperatures refer to conventional ovens. For fan-assisted ovens, please check the manufacturer's instruction manual.

DEGREES C	DEGREES F	GAS MARK
100	200	low
110	225	¼
120	250	½
140	275	1
150	300	2
160	325	3
180	350	4
190	375	5
200	400	6
220	425	7
230	450	8
250	475	9

Dry measurements

METRIC	IMPERIAL
15g	½oz
30g	1oz
60g	2oz
90g	3oz
125g	4oz (¼lb)
155g	5oz
185g	6oz
220g	7oz
250g	8oz (½lb)
280g	9oz
315g	10oz
345g	11oz
375g	12oz (¾lb)
410g	13oz
440g	14oz
470g	15oz
500g	16oz (1lb)

Liquid measurements

METRIC	IMPERIAL	US CUPS
30ml	1fl oz	⅛ cup
60ml	2fl oz	¼ cup
90ml	3fl oz	⅜ cup
120ml	4fl oz	½ cup
140ml	5fl oz	⅔ cup
170ml	6fl oz	¾ cup
200ml	7fl oz	⅞ cup
230ml	8fl oz	1 cup
260ml	9fl oz	1⅛ cups
290ml	10fl oz	1¼ cups
500ml	17½fl oz	2 cups
600ml	20fl oz	2½ cups
1 litre	1¾ pints	4 cups

Sugarpaste: recommended quantities

Always make sure you have enough sugarpaste for the size of cake you are making. This table gives the quantities required for various sizes of round and square cakes (approximate depth 3"). Remember to add extra paste if you are also covering the cake boards.

SIZE	ROUND	SQUARE
15cm (6")	450g (1lb)	570g (1¼lb)
18cm (7")	570g (1¼lb)	800g (1¾lb)
20cm (8")	800g (1¾lb)	900g (2lb)
23cm (9")	900g (2lb)	1.2kg (2½lb)
25.5cm (10")	1.2kg (2½lb)	1.4kg (3lb)
28cm (11")	1.4kg (3lb)	1.7kg (3¾lb)
30.5cm (12")	1.7kg (3¾lb)	1.8kg (4lb)
33cm (13")	1.8kg (4lb)	1.9kg (4¼lb)
35.5cm (14")	1.9kg (4¼lb)	2kg (4½lb)

Portion guide

When deciding how many portions of cake you will need, take into consideration the following sets of people: guests attending the celebration; guests attending the evening function; guests unable to attend and others not invited to whom cake will be given or posted.

A rich fruit cake will yield the most portions as it is firm and will cut into small pieces without crumbling. Madeira and similar cakes have a less dense texture and need to be cut into larger portions to prevent it breaking up.

The blue figures represent 2.5cm (1") square or 4cm x 1.5cm (1½" x ½") portions of fruit cake, and the red figures represent 5cm x 2.5cm (2" x 1") portions of Madeira/sponge cake.

SIZE	SQUARE	ROUND, TREFOIL	HEART, HEXAGON*, PETAL, OCTAGON*
15cm (6")	35 / 17	24 / 12	15 / 8
18cm (7")	47 / 24	35 / 17	24 / 12
20cm (8")	60 / 30	47 / 24	35 / 17
23cm (9")	75 / 38	60 / 30	47 / 24
25.5cm (10")	95 / 48	75 / 38	60 / 30
28cm (11")	118 / 58	95 / 48	75 / 38
30.5cm (12")	140 / 70	118 / 58	95 / 48
33cm (13")	160 / 80	140 / 70	118 / 58
35.5cm (14")	188 / 95	160 / 80	140 / 70
38cm (15")	218 / 110	188 / 95	–
40.5cm (16")	–	218 / 110	–

*Point to point

Ribbon chart

These measurements can be used to help calculate how much ribbon (in cm) will be needed to go around a cake or board. Please note that the oval has been measured at its widest point.

SIZE	ROUND	SQUARE	HEXAGON	HEART	PETAL	OVAL
15cm (6")	49	61	43	49	49	-
18cm (7")	57	72	56	56	58	-
20cm (8")	65	82	62	67	66	58
23cm (9")	73	92	70	72	72	67
25.5cm (10")	80	102	77	79	81	75
28cm (11")	89	112	86	87	87	83
30.5cm (12")	97	121	94	96	97	91
33cm (13")	105	132	101	110	104	98
35.5cm (14")	113	143	109	120	111	106
38cm (15")	121	153	115	124	120	114
40.5cm (16")	129	160	123	133	126	122

Cake by Elizabeth Finch

design ideas

SQUIRES KITCHEN
International School

about us

Squires Kitchen began in Beverley's kitchen in 1984. Beverley started baking and decorating cakes for sale, but soon realised that it was the business side of the venture that appealed to her. First the shop was opened in Wrecclesham Potteries, Surrey, in 1987, and shortly afterwards the school was set up in the family's home kitchen. As interest snowballed and customers and students came from a wide distance, new products were developed to meet customers' creative demands. Over 25 years later, Squires Kitchen's School is the largest and one of the most popular schools of its kind in the UK and is located at The Grange, a beautiful Georgian-style building in Farnham, Surrey.

Whilst we offer a professional service, it's our family feel and homely approach that keeps students coming back to Squires Kitchen's School time and time again. We've inspired many sugarcrafters, cake makers and cake decorators who came to learn with us and have now gone on to be very successful in their fields.

We enjoy meeting our students and discovering amazing talent, so we hope to see you soon on a course at Squires Kitchen.

FOR MORE INFORMATION
Contact the Course Co-ordinator at Squires Kitchen International School of Cake Decorating and Sugarcraft,
The Grange, Hones Yard, Farnham, Surrey, GU9 8BB, UK.
Tel: 0845 61 71 812 (UK, local call charges apply), +44 (0)1252 260 262 (outside UK).
See our full course list and book courses online at www.squires-school.co.uk.

the school

The Confidence to Create

At Squires Kitchen, we believe anyone can make and decorate a cake, or create beautiful sugar flowers and elegant chocolates just like a professional. Whether you bake for business or pleasure, you've come to the right place to give you the Confidence to Create.

The cookery school is used to hold demonstrations by guest authors, celebrity chefs and food stylists.

Sugarcraft

Learn everything from covering a cake to piping, modelling and making sugar flowers.

Chocolate

Discover how to make chocolates, desserts and cakes like the professionals.

Cookery

Become a domestic god or goddess by learning how to bake delicious cakes, biscuits, speciality breads and pastries.

a typical course day

A day at the Squires Kitchen School starts at 9.30am in the sugarcraft school and 10.00am in the cookery school. We suggest you arrive around 30 minutes earlier so you can collect any pre-ordered equipment, meet your tutor and classmates, get set up and have a cup of tea!

When you arrive at The Grange, turn right into the reception area to sign in and to be shown to your class. A workspace will be set up ready for you with a badge for you to write your name on.

After a brief introduction, you will get started on your course.

There will be lots of chances to ask your tutor questions should you have them, and regular breaks for refreshments.

At around 12:30pm you will break for lunch for approximately 45 minutes. Lunch will be provided in the refreshment area, where you can sit and browse through Squires Kitchen magazines and books to get plenty of ideas and inspiration! Some students choose to bring a packed lunch with them, or you may like to take a short walk by the nearby river in Gostrey Meadow. You can also visit the local shops, cafés and pubs for a bite to eat.

After lunch you'll return to the classroom for the afternoon where your class will continue until 4pm. Once you've completed your course you can take the opportunity to walk around and see what your classmates have produced and chat to the tutor if you have any questions.

the tutors

At Squires Kitchen we work with a fabulous team of regular tutors who are the very best in their specialist areas, ensuring you get expert guidance every step of the way. Not only are they great teachers, they are lovely people who will share with you their vast experience and tricks of the trade, giving you the confidence to bake, make and decorate like a professional.

We also feature guest tutors on a regular basis, so please do check our website or give us a call if you are looking for someone specific.

our Specialities: sugarcraft

If you've always wondered how to achieve super-smooth icing or how to make pretty sugar flowers for your cakes, then a Squires Kitchen sugarcraft course is for you.

At Squires Kitchen we have been teaching the art of sugarcraft for over 25 years. When you join us, you will learn all the skills and techniques you need to further your hobby, profession or passion.

We have courses suitable for everyone from the beginner to the advanced sugarcrafter.

Would you prefer individual tuition? Get in touch with us and we will arrange a personal class for you.

5 Day School with Expert Tutors

This course offers a unique opportunity to work with five different experts, each with their own specialist skills and style. Over the five days, you will learn about flower making, modelling, royal icing, sugarpaste and chocolate. On completion of the course, you will have a very good understanding of the craft and the confidence to further your sugarcraft abilities, whether it is for personal or professional purposes.

Advanced Sugar Flowers

If you already have intermediate sugar flower skills then you can build on and advance them with this course. You will learn how to make highly realistic sugar flowers with world-leading sugarcraft designer, author, teacher and demonstrator, Alan Dunn. Different flowers will be made in each class. If you've previously taken Intermediate Sugar Flowers and would like to progress then this course is the recommended next step. This class is always very popular, so we advise early booking to avoid disappointment.

Beginners' Sugar Flowers

The ability to create flowers in sugar is extremely rewarding and enables you create wonderful cake decorations for all occasions. With expert guidance, you will learn how to make a realistic display of flowers and foliage and wire them into a simple arrangement, perfect for a celebration cake. The course will cover all the necessary techniques, processes and methodology. Varying flowers will be made on each course; please check the website for further details.

Beginners' Royal Icing

This class will be an introduction to skills and techniques which form the foundation for royal iced work. We will teach you how to cover a cake with marzipan and royal icing to a smooth, professional standard. You will then learn how to decorate with simple run-outs and piping designs. You will leave the course with a real sense of achievement and the confidence to decorate with royal icing.

Beginners' Sugar Modelling

Author and novelty modelling expert Jan Clement-May will teach you the secrets of modelling animals and figures and inspire you with some wonderful children's party ideas. You will learn the basic skills and techniques needed to create novelty characters and themes suitable for cupcakes, cookies or large celebration cakes. The courses have different themes; please check the website for further details.

Beginners' Sugarpaste

If you would like to learn the skills needed to cover cakes to a professional finish and the know-how to use basic sugarcraft equipment, this is an essential course for you. Using a 6" round fruit cake you will be taught how to cover it with marzipan and sugarpaste and how to decorate it using various techniques. You will leave with the confidence to create simple and impressive celebration cakes.

Intermediate Royal Icing

If you already have basic royal icing skills then you can build on and develop them with this course. Royal icing expert, Ceri Griffiths, will introduce you to more advanced techniques including line work, inscriptions, extension piping and lace pieces. You will leave the course with a new library of skills to fine tune and develop towards advanced royal icing. If you've previously taken Beginners' Royal Icing and would like to progress then this course is the recommended next step.

Intermediate Sugar Flowers

If you already have basic sugar flower skills then you can build on and develop them with this course. With the benefit of expert guidance you will produce realistic, life-sized flowers to enhance any celebration cake for a special occasion. If you've previously taken Beginners' Sugar Flowers and would like to progress then this course is the recommended next step. Different flowers will be made on each course; please check the website for further details.

Intermediate Sugar Modelling

If you have experience in novelty modelling and would like to learn some more advanced techniques, then this course is for you. You will further develop the basic skills and techniques you have acquired to create children's party themes and bride and groom characters. Please check the website for further information regarding the topics covered on each course.

Masterclass in Royal Icing

On this fascinating three-day course, Eddie Spence MBE will teach you the secrets of royal icing and more advanced skills. Eddie will focus on a different aspect of royal icing each day, working towards a final article. The topics covered will be extension and bridge work, scrolls, run-outs, brush embroidery and lettering. This course is for students with previous royal icing and piping experience, including the coating of cakes.

Couture Cupcakes

Learn chic and contemporary cupcake decoration for all occasions. Come and find out how to create unique cupcake designs to impress using sugarpaste and the latest moulds and cutters on the market. Learn about various modelling and flower pastes as well as the use of different food colours and discover how to use texture mats, moulds, cutters and stencils like the experts.

Miniature Celebration Cakes

Individual miniature cakes are a popular choice for many occasions including children's parties, birthdays, dinner parties, weddings and Christmas. On this course we will cover ideas and designs that will incorporate many different skills including piping, modelling and the use of moulds. You will also learn how to use textured rolling pins and butterfly and flower cutters which add a beautiful finish to special occasion cakes.

Modelling with Carlos Lischetti

Join expert pastry chef and contributor to *Cakes & Sugarcraft*, Carlos Lischetti, on this course where he will shine an exciting new light on the art of sugar modelling. Carlos uses simple shapes formed from sugar modelling paste to create contemporary, striking characters that can adorn your cake on a special occasion. Carlos teaches at both beginners' and advanced level; please check our website for details.

Professional Intensive Week of Cake Decorating

Over the six days of this fast-track, professional course you will undertake in-depth theory and practical work learning about marzipan, royal icing, sugarpaste, sugar flowers and pastillage. On completion of the course, you will have a good understanding of the craft and the confidence to further your sugarcraft abilities for personal or professional purposes. Students will achieve their SK Master Certificate.

Professional Wedding Cake Course

With Paddi's expert guidance, you will design and make your own individual, tiered, sugarpasted wedding cake with a colour-coordinated wired spray of calla lilies, jasmine and foliage. Paddi will teach you a variety of techniques and skills to decorate the top and sides of the cake including appliqué, piping, sugar embroidery and the use of moulds. Some previous experience in cake decorating would be advantageous.

Starting a Cake Business from Home

Once you have experienced the satisfaction of making and decorating a cake, you may feel that you would like to take a step forward and sell your cakes from home. There are many factors to consider and Kathy Moore will help you in organising your thoughts and guide you through putting your business plan in place. Kathy will cover marketing, finance, health regulations, costing and lots more.

Stencilling Techniques

Stencilling is a fascinating technique with multiple uses. This class will introduce you to a whole new world of cake decoration and embellishment which adapts beautifully to sugarcraft. In this class you will learn how to create free-standing stencilled pieces, quick inscriptions and motifs, and be introduced to a whole new world of embellishments for cakes.

Writing and Lettering

Whether you royal ice your cakes in the traditional way or opt for a sugarpaste covering, piped greetings will add a professional touch to any celebration cake. On this course you will learn the techniques and skills involved in producing beautiful inscriptions on cakes, from how to fill a piping bag to the correct consistency for your icing. You will be shown how to pipe directly onto a cake and will also be shown invaluable tips to perfect your writing skills.

our specialities: chocolate

Squires Kitchen's chocolate courses have been carefully developed to teach you all the skills and techniques you will need to master the art of chocolate. Once you know how, you will be able to make stunning chocolates like a professional.

Would you like to know how to make delicious desserts for dinner parties, or how to make chocolate gifts for friends and family? Perhaps you are a patisserie chef who wants to brush up on skills and learn new techniques, or maybe you run your own shop. Whatever your motivation, we have a course for you.

One of our talented chocolate tutors is Mark Tilling, Squires Kitchen's Master Chocolatier and UK Chocolate Master 2006-2010. When you come on a course with Mark, he will give you a brief history of chocolate from bean to bar, explaining how this fascinating medium behaves and how to handle it like an expert. Our chocolate courses teach you everything from tempering, transfers and truffles to making decorations, desserts and showpieces. Find out how to colour chocolate, how to make ganache and how to create beautiful chocolate wedding cakes.

3 Day Professional Chocolate Wedding Cake

Design, make and decorate a two-tiered chocolate wedding cake with the expert guidance of Squires Kitchen's Master Chocolatier, Mark Tilling. You will learn and use new and contemporary techniques including how to make chocolate sponges and fillings; using syrup alcohol flavourings; the science of working with chocolate; storing chocolate; shelf life; and planning guidelines for making professional chocolate cakes.

5 Day Chocolate School

Join Mark Tilling, UK Chocolate Master 2006-2010, in mastering the art of chocolate using the finest ingredients and techniques to achieve a professional finish. Mark will take you through five days of advanced techniques including tempering and making intricate garnishes such as fans, panels, flowers and cigarillos. He will also show you how to marble with chocolate using colours, use transfer sheets and make chocolate truffles and moulded chocolates. You will produce a mini showpiece of a professional standard. You will also learn how to make different sponge chocolate cakes for weddings and special occasions, impressive desserts for dinner parties or events, and lots more chocolate goodies. Mark's teaching style is relaxed and fun and you will go home with the knowledge and skills to make your very own cakes, desserts and chocolate treats.

Chocolate for Beginners

Make beautiful, seasonal chocolate decorations for wedding and celebration cakes, cupcakes and desserts. Mark Tilling will give you a brief history of chocolate and cover the transition from bean to bar. Topics covered will include tempering, piping chocolate, designs and how to use transfer sheets to create amazing chocolate decorations. You will take home the skills to make your very own chocolate creations.

Baking with Chocolate

Make great chocolate cakes and become the envy of all your friends and family! Come along to see how to achieve delicious chocolate recipes with ganache toppings. Master Chocolatier Mark Tilling will take you through the stages of successful chocolate baking. You will make the ever-popular chocolate fudge cake, a Sachertorte, and chocolate brownies. Mark's teaching style is relaxed and fun and you will go home with the knowledge and skills to make your very own delicious cakes.

Chocolate Desserts

Join us for two days and learn how make delicious chocolate desserts that you can show off at dinner parties and share with family and friends. Learn the art of the perfect chocolate fondant and a mini assiette of chocolate desserts. Mark Tilling will take you step-by-step through making all the chocolate recipes and you will also learn the art of tempering, using transfer sheets, making chocolate mousse, sauces and a chocolate parfait. You will go home with the skills to make your very own delicious desserts.

Chocolate Modelling

Join Mark Tilling, Master Chocolatier at Squires Kitchen, for a day of working with Cocoform, a chocolate modelling paste. Mark will reveal how to colour and shape Cocoform to make different decorations for wedding and celebration cakes including fans, bows and roses. You will also learn the secret behind using Cocoform to make wonderfully delicate flowers.

Masterclass in Chocolate

Master the art of chocolate using the finest ingredients and techniques to achieve a professional finish. Over three days you will learn advanced techniques including: tempering; making garnishes such as fans, panels, flowers and cigarillos; marbling with chocolate; and using colours. You will produce a mini showpiece of a professional standard and make decadent desserts and filled chocolates and truffles.

Mini Showpiece Course

Lean how to make amazing showpieces with Mark Tilling, UK Chocolate Master 2006-2010. On this course you will design and create a chocolate showpiece. You will learn about chocolate and how to work with it like a professional. Learn how to temper chocolate, use transfer sheets and how to decorate with different cocoa butter colours. You will take home your own chocolate showpieces and an array of new skills.

Miniature Chocolate Cakes

Individual miniature cakes are a popular choice for many occasions. Come and learn how they are made with Mark Tilling, Squires Kitchen's Master Chocolatier. This beginners' course will cover ideas and designs that incorporate many different skills including piped flowers, modelling, moulds, transfers and much more. Impress your guests with these delightful miniature cakes.

Moulded Chocolates and Truffles

Learn how to make contemporary styled chocolates and truffles. The course will include: how to temper chocolate; make ganaches and caramels; the use of chocolate moulds; how to dip chocolates and roll truffles; use cocoa butter colours and different piping techniques. What's more, you can take home everything you make as well as the recipes. This course is offered at both basic and advanced level; check the website for further details.

Chocolate Special

Make beautiful, seasonal chocolate decorations for wedding and celebration cakes, cupcakes and desserts. Mark will give you a brief history of chocolate including the transition from bean to bar. Topics covered will include tempering, piping chocolate designs and how to use transfer sheets to create amazing chocolate decorations. You will take home the skills to make your own chocolate creations.

our Specialities: cookery

Now you can bake your cake as well as decorate it at Squires Kitchen.

Let's go back to the very beginning – learning how to make cakes, pastries and breads from scratch. Once you know the basics of beautiful baking you'll be able to create recipes to suit your project, introducing new flavours, filings and toppings.

Learn how to master favourite recipes such as Victoria sponge, gingerbread and chocolate cakes, and how to bake the best cupcakes and special occasion cakes.

Our cookery classes are taught by top food stylists and patissiers, as well as guest authors and celebrity chefs.

5 Day Baking School

Join Mark Tilling for this intensive five-day baking course. Learn all you need to know about baking bread, cakes, pastries and lots more. With an impressive CV including head pastry chef at leading hotels, Mark will pass on numerous skills he has learnt over the years. Over the five days you will learn about different pastries (puff, choux and sweet) and how to use them to make tarts and mini sweet pastries. You will make artisan breads, sponge cakes, fruit cakes and delicious chocolate sponges, and will learn the art of the French pastry chef. Mark's teaching style is relaxed and fun and you will go home with the knowledge and skills to make your very own baked treats.

Baking for Cake Decorating

Spend two days making cakes that are suitable for stacking and carving and create different fillings for all occasions. Join Mark Tilling in making different sponge and fruit cakes that would be ideal as wedding cakes. The cakes you will make include rich fruit cake, boiled fruit cake, Genoise, Madeira and chocolate cakes. Mark will also show you different fillings that would go with the different sponges and will also teach you how to stack cakes. We recommend following this course with Beginners' Sugarpaste, in which you will be able to decorate one of your cakes.

Basic Bread Making

Learn the art of making bread from scratch for irresistible results. We will teach you how to bake classic breads without a bread making machine in sight. Come and learn the best ways of making bread using fresh and dried yeasts as well as different flours and flavours. After learning the skills of kneading and shaping breads, you will make a classic white cottage loaf, wholemeal rolls, rosemary and olive oil focaccia and rye bread.

Bread Making

Learn the art of bread making the way it should be made! We will teach you how to bake classic breads without a breadmaker in sight. Come and learn the best ways of making bread using fresh and dried yeasts and different flours and flavours. Make a classic white cottage loaf, wholemeal rolls, rosemary and olive oil focaccia, rye, soda, apple and sultana, brioche and sourdough breads. Learn the skills of kneading and shaping breads for irresistible results.

Christmas Baking Special

Come and join Mark Tilling to make delicious fruit cake, Christmas pudding and chocolate Yule log for the festive season. Once you have the skills you can create your own baked goodies all year round. Learn how to make a classic baked fruit cake for Christmas that can also be used for weddings, christenings, birthdays or any other special occasion. You will also have the chance to make a fruity steamed Christmas pudding and a delicious chocolate Yule log with Christmas decoration. Mark's teaching style is relaxed and fun and you will go home with the knowledge and skills to make a delicious festive feast.

Christmas Inspiration Week

Celebrate the season and get your Christmas preparations underway with this special selection of baking and chocolate courses. Join us and be inspired for anything between one and all five days of this festive week! Each day will bring a different skill to the foreground, be it the baking skills to make a perfect Christmas pudding or the skills to make a Christmas fruit cake. Visit the website for further information regarding individual subjects to be covered.

Baking Cupcakes

Develop your cupcake skills with contemporary ideas to create fantastic and loveable cakes for any celebration. You will have the choice of making a variety of chocolate or lemon cupcakes to top with lemon icing and rose petals, piped butterflies and pretty piped flowers.

French Pâtisserie

Learn the art of French pâtisserie on this three-day course. We will teach you how to make the delicious pastries that grace the windows of French pâtisseries in your own kitchen. Mark Tilling will teach you how to make choux, puff and sweet pastries; bake mini tarts, mousses, cakes and macaroons; and make French classics such as gateau St. Honoré and gateau opera. Mark's teaching style is relaxed and fun and you will go home with the knowledge and skills to make your very own French pastries.

Fruit Cakes Uncovered

Come and join Mark Tilling to make delectable fruit cakes. This course will cover all the skills that you will need to make three different fruit cakes to use for any special occasion. Learn how to make a classic baked fruit cake for use at weddings, christenings or birthdays. You will also have the chance to make a boiled fruit cake and an afternoon tea fruit cake, ideal for any occasion.

Marvellous Meringues

Discover how to make meringues to professional standards. Learn new ways of piping and shaping meringues and find out how to make contemporary designs in different ways, from piping and moulding to adding flavours and colours. You will also see the difference between using fresh and powdered egg whites.

Macaroons Made Easy

Macaroons have made a huge comeback, appearing in the chicest of bakeries everywhere. Mark Tilling will show you how to make macaroons with the perfect taste and texture using a wide variety of flavour and colour combinations so your macaroons will look and taste absolutely irresistible. With an impressive CV including head pastry chef at leading hotels, Mark will also show you how to decorate them with a professional finish so that you can create stunning displays and personalised gifts.

Muffins with Cookie Bellair

Come and join *Cakes & Sugarcraft* columnist, Cookie Bellair, to learn how to make fabulous home-baked muffins. Cookie will reveal her favourite tried-and-tested basic muffin recipe, with delicious variations. The course will also include flapjacks and vanilla fancies and you will be able to add your own signature to what you make. Cookie's enthusiasm for cookery and creative flair combine to make this an enjoyable day filled with new ideas and plenty of fun.

Perfect Pastry

Learn how to make the perfect homemade pastry and become the envy of all your friends. With an impressive CV including head pastry chef at leading hotels, Mark Tilling will pass on numerous skills he has learnt over the years. You will learn about different types of pastry, their uses, and the techniques that you need to ensure fantastic results every time. After making different pastries, you will turn them into delicious apple pie, lemon meringue pie and profiteroles with chocolate sauce.

Perfect Sponge Cakes

Wouldn't we all like to make cakes like grandma did? Come along to see how to achieve the best results for delicious, classic cakes. Mark Tilling will take you through the stages of successful baking. You will make a traditional Victoria sponge which will be so light and fluffy, you won't believe that you made it! You will also make a mouth-wateringly gooey carrot cake covered in a creamy light topping, and a wonderful apple cake that is spicy and sweet.

Summer Wedding Cupcakes

Cupcakes and mini cakes are still a massive wedding trend and are so incredibly versatile. With expert guidance you will develop your cupcake skills with contemporary ideas to create these fantastic little cakes for weddings and other celebrations. After baking beautifully light sponges you will top them with fondants, fruits and flowers and discover new ways of design and decoration.

Tempting Tarts

Join Mark Tilling in making the best sweet tarts in the world; learn how to make sweet pastries and shortcrust pastry from scratch to make delicious tarts for all occasions. Mark will teach you step-by-step how to make the perfect sweet pastry and shortcrust pastry. You will make a sweet apple tart, raspberry frangipane tart and a roasted savoury quiche. Learn skills of blind baking and decorating using moulds.

name   **address/email**   **phone**

name	address/email	phone

name   address/email   phone

👥 name	📧 address/email	☎ phone

SQUIRES KITCHEN

Squires Kitchen Sugarcraft Ltd.
Squires Kitchen is the original company formed in 1984. This includes a retail
outlet in Farnham, Surrey, factory and warehousing units in Hampshire where
specialist food colourings and sugars are manufactured for distribution to the
sugarcraft industry, Squires Kitchen's mail-order company and the online shop.
Come and visit the Squires Kitchen shop at
3 Waverley Lane, Farnham, Surrey, GU9 8BB, UK.
Order online at www.squires-shop.com.
To contact our Customer Services team, please email
customer@squires-shop.com
or call 0845 61 71 810 (or +44 1252 260 260 from outside the UK).

Squires Kitchen's International School
Squires Kitchen's School has been teaching the art of cake decorating
and sugarcraft since 1987. The school was created to share our extensive
knowledge of the craft with the help of amazing teachers and passionate
students.
In spring 2010, Squires Kitchen's sugarcraft school relocated to larger
premises at The Grange, a beautiful Georgian style building close by. Next door
is the new cookery school, a fully equipped room complete with state-of-the-art
appliances from Smeg, so you can come to Squires to learn everything from
baking a cake to decorating it.
View and book courses at www.squires-school.co.uk.
To contact our Course Co-ordinator, please email
school@squires-shop.com
or call 0845 61 71 812 (or +44 1252 260 262 from outside the UK).

B. Dutton Publishing Ltd. and Squires Kitchen Magazine Publishing (SKMP)
B. Dutton Publishing Ltd. are publishers of high quality craft and cake
decoration books and magazines. Working with many of the top names in
sugarcraft, we have a growing portfolio of books that are sold all over the world.
We also publish glossy consumer magazines under our subsidiary, SKMP,
including *Cakes & Sugarcraft*, *Wedding Cakes – A Design Source*, and *Inspired
by Food*. SKMP titles are distributed in over 30 countries worldwide.
All of our publications and magazine subscriptions can be ordered online at
www.squires-shop.com.
To contact our Customer Services team, please email
customer@squires-shop.com
or call 0845 61 71 810 (or +44 1252 260 260 from outside the UK).

Squires Kitchen, The Grange, Hones Yard, Farnham, Surrey, GU9 8BB
www.squires-shop.com
www.facebook.com/squireskitchenuk
www.twitter.com/squireskitchen